ONE GIRL, FOUR STEI   LESSONS

the

NAKED
EXECUTIVE

HOW BEING HONEST CAN
CHANGE YOUR LIFE *Forever*

KELLY DAVIES

MORGAN JAMES PUBLISHING • NEW YORK

the NAKED EXECUTIVE

ISBN: 978-1-61448-073-0 (Paperback)
Library of Congress Control Number: 2010934411

Published by:
MORGAN JAMES PUBLISHING
1225 Franklin Ave Ste 32
Garden City, NY 11530-1693
Toll Free 800-485-4943
www.MorganJamesPublishing.com

Logo Design by:
Barry Armstrong
barry@armstrongco.net

Cover/Interior Design by:
Rachel Lopez
rachel@r2cdesign.com

Find out who you are and do it on purpose.
—DOLLY PARTON

preface

I n this book, may you find a safe place to say your life isn't perfect.

May you find a safe place to say you feel like a failure, you're sick of being busy and numb all the time.

May you find a safe place to know that the truth won't kill you, but living a lie might.

May you find the courage to join the Naked Movement and live a naked life: honest in your thoughts, action and words.

It will change everything.

contents

introduction

MY FIRST TIME GETTING NAKED

Do you remember your first time getting naked? I will never forget mine. It was during my last year of graduate school, fall semester of 2009.

Graduate school was a life changing experience for me. My program was in Executive Leadership and Organizational Change. We did an intense study of emotional intelligence and right at the very top of the list of competencies was a biggie, "self-awareness." All the students in the program were successful and experienced professionals, we knew what self awareness is (or so we thought). Ironically, in a program on leadership, we had no defined leadership roles. We worked in teams and those leadership roles were delegated out on a project and task basis. There was no seniority, no titles and no get out of jail free cards. We were learning to "learn" and trying not to "perform" but its tough for successful type A's to not want to perform. We had spent our entire lives performing for others to gain power, prestige and position, those things that raises and promotions are made of.

In year two, we worked with a new team, which means we tried to 'prove' ourselves all over again. We gave each other feedback after each weekend of classes on how we contributed to the team and on our leadership contribution. We also completed a reflection paper of at least 10 pages that forced us to reflect on what we had learned, about ourselves and others, which included examples. This was a major part of our grade in the program. At this point in the program, I was still performing. I was numb to my "closed off" self, because I am a really nice and perky person. One of my classmates told me his first impression of me was that there was no way this little blonde cheerleader was going to make it through this program (after I announced to the class during orientation that I wanted to change the world as we knew it).

During the fall of 2009 things were rough personally, I was having a personal meltdown, I think. I was running through the holidays and then I spent New Year's Eve crying on the couch reading Buddhist philosophy on being content with what is (through very discontented tears) and I truly wondered, "why in the world am I here? Why in the world did I enter this graduate program?" I thought, "I am insane and several people agree. I have a great career, I have a fantastic son, why can't I just give it up and quit searching for 'that' thing?"

Our team had a huge project due on Saturday morning. We had a thirty-minute complete strategic presentation to real venture capital guys to get 6 million fake dollars to invest in our simulation company we were running for the semester. It was a big deal. I was in the throes of a work crisis with clients, I had been on the road and it was Thursday night at 10 pm and I was just settling down to start reviewing the information. I was supposed to leave for school in less than 12 hours. I was exhausted. I had a choice: either stay up until at least 3 am (again) and crash to prepare to make a minor contribution to the team project and pretend that I am well prepared, or be honest with the team, let them know where I am and what I can do. I realized that I would be saying, "I know, I suck, you guys got stuck with the worst team member in the program that lives 4 hours away and now you will have to pull my weight." But I was so tired, so I closed my eyes and sent the team an email:

Guys, I have to be honest, I'm really struggling right now. I've been on the road nonstop, and just haven't been able to dig into the simulation material and prepare for the presentation like I would like. I feel really bad and like I have let the team down, but please know I will participate in any way that I can, I'm happy to present anything you put together for me. I'm sorry, I'll make a better contribution to our next project.

I wanted to throw up when I hit send at 11 pm. I had admitted to the team that I sucked, that I hadn't been able to prepare, and that I wasn't a superhero. I waited to be struck by lightening or for a mythical figure very similar to the death eaters from the Harry Potter series to swoop instantly into my bedroom and to suck my unworthy soul from my body.

I had been hypersensitive to my long distance commute since the program began. I was the only person that attended from out of town. Every one else was local, which allowed the teams to get together and work on things on a very casual and impromptu basis. Our team couldn't do that. We had to do conference calls and video conferencing. I felt bad about it. I felt I was an inconvenience to the team. This was my worst fear, come true. I had to rely on someone else completely. Could I trust them? Would they be snarky behind my back to class members? Would they trash my contribution in their reflection papers that the professors would read? Basically, I was prepared for my entire reputation to be shredded. I would be an intellectual outcast, barely worthy of being in the program.

I got two immediate emails back from team members: "no worries, we've got your back" and, "we've got it covered, be careful on your drive." I was shocked. I didn't really expect to hear much back from them. I expected that they would, of course, talk to each other about my lack of performance, but not talk to me about it.

I was shocked, "this was their response?" Where were the death eaters? There was an enormous burden lifted from my shoulders. I let my wall down and trusted these guys with the truth and they actually supported me. Believe me, I thought about several huge lies I could have told the team about why I couldn't get something done. I thought about being sick that weekend and having to stay home with great remorse and regret that I couldn't help the team. I was just tired of trying to think of lies.

After this project, we grew much closer as a team. By being honest with them about my struggles, it gave them permission to be honest about their own as well, and I felt something very new and different. I later found out that feeling was love and compassion.

I saw hope in humans. Perhaps, just maybe, everyone is not out to get me, maybe everyone won't hurt me. Maybe, just maybe, I could let love in, and that was my real first time. That was the first time I let myself be human. That's how the naked movement began. One girl who decided she was tired of pretending that her life was always fantastic, that she didn't need to rely on anyone for anything, and she could do pretty much anything at anytime for anyone and smile while holding it all together. She finally cracked wide open and like the "Grinch who Stole Christmas," her "heart grew three sizes that day."

In this book, I am naked. This event with my team felt so incredible that I made the decision to live a naked life from then on, to be honest in my thoughts, actions and words. At the time I didn't realize the unconscious processes that we go through when we are making the decision to trust others enough to get naked with them. I also didn't realize that there were several very important lessons that I would learn as I was getting and staying naked, but I know them now.

Throughout this book, I want you to know me so that you can know you. I will share a very simple four-step process that you can use each and every time you find yourself in a situation where you think, "do I tell the truth or just let this slide because it's more convenient?" Each time you let things slide you are unconsciously telling yourself that someone else is more important and more worthy than yourself. I will walk you through this process in great detail so that you will become an expert at telling anyone the truth about anything.

I also want you to benefit from the lessons I have learned the hard way. These lessons were learned through experience, not some theory in a book. You will meet friends and family members that decided to begin telling the truth, their own truths, no matter how uncomfortable. I will share why I think the lessons are important and how to know which lesson you might be learning and the benefits of pushing through it.

You have committed to being naked. Now what? The benefits of being naked are numerous. You will spend less time and energy on the "waffles," which is the vicious cycle of should have's and could have's. You will spend less time in dead end relationships that are sucking the life out of you. Perhaps most importantly you will decide who you really are and what you truly like.

Being naked empowers you to make the decisions that you want. These may not be the decisions your parents want, the decisions your spouse wants or the decisions that television, movies and media are always selling you. Who cares? You will start getting naked by making small personal decisions, just for you. These small decisions, such as wearing your favorite color, will create momentum to achieve other goals that you may set, whether it be a job change, a relationship do-over or a twenty pound weight loss. Aren't you tired of setting a goal and never hitting it? Aren't you tired of starting a project and never finishing it? We don't finish those things that we aren't committed to and by getting naked, you choose to commit.

We committed to being honest and that changed everything.

This book isn't perfect, and neither am I. A naked life is one that is always in progress and that's where I am, a work in progress.

You will find things in this book you agree with, and things you vehemently disagree with, which is fantastic. In order to know who you are, you must decide what you are about. Too often we decide who we are by process of elimination, eliminating what we don't like. I suspect you are much more familiar with what you hate than what you love, but you won't be for long.

Enjoy the book, enjoy the process and remember Lesson # 5: Everything just feels better naked.

CHAPTER 1

NAKED 101:
THE BASICS

I realize that most books have all of the Q and A at the end, after you've read the book. This book is different. I know you are puzzled right now. You sorta understand naked, you kinda understand that you think you might need to get a little naked, but you're really not quite sure about this whole "naked" thing. So I decided to add the questions to the front of the book, because it just felt like the right thing to do and that's part of being naked, not being afraid to do something unusual or unconventional because it's not the way it's usually done. Prepare for a lot of naked in this book.

WHAT IS NAKED?

It's really simple: Naked is being honest in your thoughts, actions and words. Naked starts as something that you do, and becomes something that you are.

What does naked look like?

A naked person is one that acknowledges themselves fully, the parts they like and dislike equally. We all have things that we dislike about ourselves. We spend time and energy trying to ignore those parts, lose those parts and exterminate those parts. They begin by showing up on every year's resolution list in the form of "I will lose 20 pounds." After the goal has been on the list for five years, we should add a more appropriate goal "quit being a person that never accomplishes these goals."

Naked people make decisions that align their mind, body and soul. This means their decisions make them more fulfilled, happier with life and more confident in themselves. How many of your decisions are doing that right now?

Naked people let themselves feel things. Let me repeat that, they FEEL things, real things, feelings, for themselves and for others. They talk about their fears and feelings because they know that by exposing them they lose all their negative power over us.

Naked people know what compassion is because they have it first for themselves which allows them to have it for others, all others, not just some others, and all the time, not just when they have the time or energy.

A naked person knows what real love is and they give it freely, with no expectations, because when you learn what real love is, you realize it cannot be taken away from you and it's always there for you if you look deep enough.

A naked person is content. Content with today, content with this moment, appreciative of the past for the lessons learned, optimistic about the future, but lives and appreciates this moment alone.

A naked person is someone that is honest, open, compassionate, loved and content. A naked person is not a super hero, above all else, a naked person is a mere human and that's how I know you want to be naked.

WHY DO I WANT TO BE NAKED?

In the beginning, as babies, we were all naked, me, you, everyone. We were content, happy, fulfilled; there was no seeking, no searching for meaning, for happiness, for your purpose, we just were. We could just be. Then something happened, and like that, in an instant, everything changed. All of the sudden, we were born into this big world we live in. If you go back even further, there is a familiar story that many of us have heard before that illustrates this state of being as well. You know, you're standing in the Garden of Eden, everything's fabulous, the birds are singing, the sun is shining. All needs are met, everything is taken care of. Adam and Eve were allowed to just be and with one action, all of the sudden, everything changed. To live is to change and many times it happens unexpectedly and we find ourselves in unfamiliar places, full of fear.

Life allows everything to change without your permission and does not necessarily follow your timeline or your game plan. You suddenly lose what you had (or think you had) with no warning whatsoever, it just disappears. Whatever your "it" was, "it" disappeared.

We all have "its," some similar, such as lovers, friends, jobs and some not so similar such as an arm in a shark attack or a college scholarship, but all of these "its," are pieces and parts of us, our souls our spirits our lives. When they disappear, we are suddenly lost. Things you cherished, the things you knew and loved, poof, all gone.

And that's what happened to me. I woke up one morning and realized that I was not happy and for the first time I admitted it. I realized that I was spending more of my life wishing for the future to get here than I was spending enjoying each day. Sure, there were highlight reels from holidays and vacations and "events" but there was no true contentment with a Monday or a Sunday. I was becoming a robot, moving from one task to the next, staying busy, equating busy with productive and successful. But when things got still, when I sat down in an attempt to rest, there was a restlessness deep down inside that I could not identify, yet could not turn off.

You are like me. You are searching for something and you don't know what it is. You're not completely content and this makes you afraid. You are afraid because you don't know what "it" is, this thing that you feel drawn toward and are working toward, yet can't name, feel or visualize. We both know it's uncomfortable and inconvenient for us to not be in total control of how we feel. This feeling of discontent creates discomfort, which we try to numb out with "stuff." Addiction to feelings, created with people, drugs, alcohol or things. Drama created with affairs, divorces, sibling rivalries, parental resentment and the most common, plain old busy. I suspect you have experience with one or more of these coping mechanisms, all of which create distraction and create layer after layer around that "thing" we cannot find.

I know you want to be naked because you are looking for that "thing." You are looking for freedom, the freedom to be your naked self.

HOW DO YOU KNOW I'M "BUSY" ALL THE TIME?

In the defense of busy, we instinctively know there is something that we are supposed to be doing, so we keep on moving. You know, the normal kind of busy we all have, responsibilities, the job, the family, the community. We fill our lives with things we think we must "do" to be who we are. The problem is we don't seem to find joy or contentment in most things that we do, so instead of passion and enthusiasm, our activity breeds discontent and many times resentment.

What happens when some of our "busy things" go away, many times without our consent? A marriage suddenly is dissolved, a job title, salary and task list are outsourced. What are you left with when those things are removed from your list of "have to dos"?

Many of us just fill the space on the list, with something, busy. We do the things that we think we are supposed to do. Look for a job that has a nice title, good salary. Become one of the many "looking for love" divorcees. But something deep inside is still aching. It is a tiny little voice that we try to ignore or stuff down. It is the voice of the true feelings of hurt and anguish, the true fears of being alone and unsuccessful.

We live in a feel good fast world. One that creates an expectation on television and in magazines that you should be able to feel good with that new car, new body or new drug. Well, I went through that list and you do feel good, for a little while. Then you have to go looking for another something: a new pair of shoes, a new wine, a new exciting friend, just so you have something to do that occupies your mind and body, and not necessarily in that order. As long as your thoughts are occupied you can't get stuck in that world where things creep in like "I'm so in debt," "there are so many things wrong with this relationship," "I don't have any true friends." We have no time or place for these kinds of thoughts, yet they are in there. They are the thoughts that live in that tiny little place that you try to ignore. They are the thoughts that your mind refuses to acknowledge that live in your heart. This is your real heart. The one that lies patiently waiting for you to defrost the ice blockade that you've been building around it for years. The layers and layers of disappointments, hurts and fears that you don't want to have to acknowledge or deal with. They are all there, waiting. It's just a matter of time before the pile gets so big, that you truly can't ignore them. You might be one of the lucky ones, you can finally have your heart broken open so wide that you have no choice but to just let it all out. I assure you, it doesn't feel like you are lucky when it is happening. It doesn't matter who, what or why it gets broken, it feels the same. Perhaps that's what shocks us the most, the feeling. It's one we've heard about, but rarely let ourselves fully feel, true pain, brokenness, gut wrenching sobbing on the floor, why did this happen to me, how did I let this happen, pain. You try all of the old familiar ways to hold things in and push through to the next feel good moment, but none of those work anymore and you are just broken open. You then have a pivotal choice to make: you either hide or you seek. You either wait a little bit and then duct tape the thing back together or you begin a journey to burn it to the ground and finally let go of everything that is in that tiny place. You slowly realize that each time you truly let yourself fully acknowledge how you feel (tears and all), you end up feeling a little lighter, a little better, a little stronger and more confident in yourself. I wish I knew what makes a person choose to hide or seek. You have this book, so you are either a seeker or trying to make the decision to come out of hiding. You're either using this book to stay busy or take a very short break from busy, either way I know you are tired of busy.

YOU ARE AS NAKED AS YOU CAN BE RIGHT NOW

In the story of Eden we find the apple, the snake and the woman. We've been trying for years to figure out whom to blame for that incident! It's a great example of how quickly things can change and we have no control and no way to go back to how things were. Adam and Eve realized they were naked, panicked and began trying to cover up. They had no choice at that point but to move on with life. Supposedly we got kicked out of that garden, but I have to admit I question this, where was free will in it all? Couldn't we have protested and stayed? You know, the first sit in? Anyway, we, like Adam and Eve, eventually must move beyond what we knew, what we were comfortable with, what we trusted, and who we always thought we were. What Adam and Eve had was freedom.

They were free to do anything they wanted, to sleep when they were sleepy, to eat when they were hungry, to play, to walk, to talk freely, they could do anything they wanted to do. I don't think that Eve was counting calories or that Adam felt any need to accumulate "riches," impress anyone with his animal naming talents, or look for something to fix around the house. There was one rule they had to obey, which God stated was for their own good. I often think about this with my teenage son. Is there anything that I could possibly say or do that would convince him to listen to some of the rules that as parents we try to have him obey, for his own safety and well-being?

It seems as humans, we are determined to learn our lessons the hard way, through experience.

How do you feel about the snake in this story? God created the snake too! Adam named it like all the other animals. Yet, the snake is the animal that tempted Eve by telling her that the reason she could not eat of "the tree" was that God didn't want her to have knowledge like he did. Then she talked Adam into it as well. That darn snake has become a symbol of many things for all of us. It is a symbol of fear for many.

Why are we so afraid of snakes? I suspect it is because they seem sneaky. They can't help it people, they are one long muscle and have NO bones. What else are they going to do besides slither? So how many of you hate snakes? How many of you have had personal harm done by a snake? How many of you cannot outrun a snake? Please, think about why you are actually afraid of a snake. If you can come up with a good reason, let me know.

How do you feel about the apple tree? According to the story, there was only one tree they couldn't eat from. They were not supposed to eat the fruit from this one tree, and it was an apple. Look at the grocery store, how many bins of apples are there? How many types of bananas? Really? Are we just gluttons for punishment? Why is the apple now our most common fruit of all? Let's summarize this story: they picked an apple, juicy, red, round, chomp, one bite, as humans, we're done. So what would have happened had she eaten the entire apple? We got knowledge with one bite, good grief I cannot image what we would have gotten if she had eaten the whole thing.

Why knowledge? Think about all the things that they could have gotten with that apple. "You've won a new car, the lottery, a year's supply of meat you don't have to kill for yourself." No, they got "Knowledge." Was this the beginning of the modern IQ test? Now they had something that could let them know how smart (or not) they were. Compared to whom? They were the only people there. I notice they did not get wisdom from eating the apple. So, they obviously were not idiots or infantile. They were capable of taking care of themselves in a jungle. They were eating, sleeping, drinking and getting along quite nicely without that "knowledge." I have a theory, you see I think they already had wisdom, it was inherent in them. What's the difference between knowledge and wisdom? You can think of wisdom as a built in GPS system. This GPS would show them safety, food, water, shelter, love. Wisdom is based on what is true and real, it was all they needed. Wisdom is doing the right thing at the right moment at the right place with the knowledge that you have.

They took a bite of the apple and then they realized they needed to cover up in a hurry. All of the sudden instead of knowing they were "thinking." Thinking of all their options, thinking about the different fruits in the garden, thinking about where they could hide. I believe at that point their minds began to recognize three new places, the past, the present and the future. They could now remember the past, when they had freedom and were free from many types of pain, they knew their present condition and they also had to look toward something new, a new land and new family members. I assume there were none of these thoughts when they were in the garden. Instead of God's voice in their heads, their heads were now filled with their own voice. Knowledge brought a host of new friends along with him, guilt, shame, distrust and betrayal. You know them all, they travel in a pack and normally all show up together.

Hmmm, shut your eyes for a moment. Imagine your life right now without any of these friends. You no longer have any guilt for what you have done or what you have not done. You have no shame in yourself. There is no reason for you to hide any piece or part of you. You trust all people, equally and openly and most importantly, you have never been betrayed. No one has ever disappointed you or not met your expectations. What does this life feel like? What would a typical day look like for you? What would you do with your time and energy? What would you complain about or obsess about? I bet your life would be much different than it is today.

So what happened to you? What happened in your life to open your eyes and make you realize that you were all covered up and buried deep? What made you realize that you're not really here? What was your apple? What did that moment feel like when everything started crashing down around you, when you saw the façade of yourself start to evaporate, to float away in a vapor so thin that you could not possibly catch it or contain it? What did you do? Where did you go? What is your apple? Maybe you know these answers and you are looking for some support to move forward. Maybe you know these answers and you have no idea what the hell you're doing. Maybe your mother or friend bought you this book because they think you don't know what the hell you're doing. Your friends might even think you are losing your mind as you start to separate yourself from those people around you that you really don't like to be around, and you stop pretending that you feel ok all the time, and you admit you are just not sure what your next steps are going to be.

So, who are you now? Why aren't you naked? Can you feel that tiny voice inside of your heart, whispering to you, encouraging you, calling to you? Like a mother's gentle voice, far in the distance, only recognized by her child, it calls to you. It calls when you are awake, when you are sleeping and eventually no amount of busyness can drown it out. And that feeling, what is that feeling? It tugs at you, it pulls you and entices you and scares you to the core. It is a voice like a whisper, so faint that you cannot make out what the words are. A voice heard gently on the wind, barely audible, yet unceasing. It calls and calls, never waning, never complaining and never leaving. Do you hear the voice telling you that you just aren't who you're supposed to be?

What is this thing that is trying to break through? A birth of sorts, of a new idea, a new era, a new something, not yet named. Perhaps you are attempting to be born again, to have another chance. A golden opportunity before it's too late. You're feeling the tug, hearing the voice, that's how I know you are as naked as you can be right now.

WHO CAN GET NAKED?

Anyone who is willing can get naked. You just have to start where you are. You must see through different eyes, the eyes of the heart. You commit to the alignment of your thoughts, actions and words. So often we think one thing and when the moment comes to reveal our authentic self, we just don't have the courage to go against the grain, to allow ourselves to stand out, to possibly not fit in. You need to know that this is a process, not a place, and that just when you think you are rocking and rolling in authentic and honest relationships, something will happen that rocks your world again, but you cannot give in or give up. That's what your naked friends are for.

WHAT DO I NEED TO KNOW BEFORE I START GETTING NAKED?

In order to get naked, you need to able to recognize wisdom and knowledge.

Remember that Adam and Eve got knowledge. Whoopie! They won the lottery, they got a whole lot of information. Listen very closely to this, it is very important: "Knowledge is information and information by itself is nothing." You can have the blueprints for a house and read them, understand them, and have knowledge of the house, but that doesn't build a house. You have knowledge of the plans, but no house.

I have always thought of myself as being pretty intelligent. I have shelves and shelves of books, I read all the time, and I tell people way too often, "I read a book about that." I thought this made me smart, but what I've learned is it gave me a lot of knowledge about topics. I was told at the beginning of my naked journey that I was actually a collector, a collector of information. I had to realize I was reading to gather information, but rarely using it. This was the primary way that I dealt with how I was feeling. If I was unsettled or uncertain, I bought a book about it to try to figure out what was going on. I was quite certain that there was someone out there who could tell me what was going on in here. I am an Amazon Prime member. Yes, I am one of those apostle customers who actually pays them money so I can order more from them, thus paying them more money (and I'm happy about it.) It's marketing genius for sure. If I don't buy something from Amazon every week, I go into withdrawal. I seriously think that my brain cells start to evaporate if I don't have at least one cardboard box on my desk a week. They are like the world's biggest library. When books are your friends and companions it is like one instant on demand party. If I'm lonely, I just find some friends in the books on Amazon. If I'm bored, I just find a new subject to study or a book on "why the hell am I bored all the time?" I love the relationship I have with Amazon. They know me, my heart and soul. Every time I sign in, they have recommendations, just for me! It's like they can read my mind and isn't that one of the things we are always looking for in a relationship? I have never been disappointed by Amazon. They have always met their commitments. How many of those books have I actually read all the way through? Hmmm, good question. As many as I needed to before I found the answer to whatever question seemed to be tormenting my soul at the moment. In other words, not many. This book is about tapping into your wisdom and building that naked muscle to hear wisdom's voice above knowledge's growl.

Wisdom is what points you in the direction of truth and eventually allows you to recognize your own truth, hopefully once and for all. It's important to recognize the difference between wisdom and knowledge and to use them both appropriately. This is key to getting naked and more importantly, staying naked. Remember that knowledge is information, only information, nothing more or less. Now wisdom, that's the other twin. Wisdom uses knowledge at the right time in the right place to create the right answers for you. FOR YOU, not for your parents, your spouse, your friends, but the right answers for you. This is where we get a little shaky. When we find ourselves on a path that we no longer recognize as our own, it's difficult to trust making authentic decisions that are right for us. Many times as we're getting naked, these right decisions are so different from the ones we have made previously that we get very little support and a lot of suspicion, speculation and flat out anger from others. You can expect this, you've had it happen many times before when you have tried to make changes in any area of your life. People are scared of people that actually do the things they say they are going to do, like change. You can become a reminder that they do not value themselves enough to actually commit to permanent change.

Wisdom is contained deep within our souls, it was breathed into our hearts as we came in to this world, this body, this life, with a purpose and a message. Like Adam and Eve, we all have a purpose, our own truth. It's what you're looking for right now and you're going to have to get naked to find it again.

We have wisdom deep inside of us and every once in a while we hear it whisper to us. That innocent child we used to be really wants us to listen to it so that we can get back on that path to our own truth, to our authentic selves. Now this would be a naked homecoming. It's not a band aid or a change of clothes, it's not a new exercise regime or the newest car model on the market. It's real change, sustainable change. It is taking steps to getting back to who you are and staying there. It's Naked, and you know what they say, "once you see someone naked, you can't go back, you never forget!"

This journey truly is simple, but it is not easy. It's a journey, an adventure to find that wisdom without hesitancy. To find yourself and to love yourself and to harness that energy and move toward your true purpose in life.

If you were looking for knowledge, just facts and information, you'd better buy another book. I suspect you're looking for the real answer, the one you've been searching for. To find your truth and live it, to trust the wisdom of the moment. I know you're searching, that's why you found me.

SO WHY HAVE SO MANY PEOPLE BECOME SO DISCONTENTED AND NOT "NAKED"?

We can thank our good old friend, knowledge. Knowledge contributes significantly to discontentment. Knowledge enters the picture and we get his cousin relativity and the crew: relativity, the ability to track time, to compare, to assume, to measure. Facts used by the ego to support the status quo.

Relativity: the art of comparisons

Let's define relative a little because it's very important. Relative means something "is" because it is compared to something else. You only know something is hot because you have an assumption of what something cold is, right? So, relative terms may include pretty, rich, healthy, famous, successful, any of these on any given day is relative, because you have to ask, "compared to what?" I am rich compared to a homeless person and not rich compared to Bill Gates. So should I say that I am rich? No, probably not. It's a relative term. According to Dan Ariely in *Predictably Irrational*, "We don't have an internal value meter that tells us how much things are worth. Rather, we focus on the relative advantage of one thing over another, and then estimate value accordingly. (For instance, we don't know how much a six-cylinder car is worth, but we can assume it's more expensive than the four-cylinder model)." As you begin to look at your true self, without any of the airbrushing and cover ups, you will expose the areas in which you have been comparing yourself to others. The goal of naked is to remove any and all props and to see who it is that is left standing with everything else taken away. Ask yourself, "how do I know this is true?" If the only way you think it is true is because you are comparing it to something else, it is probably not true. It is from this naked point that we can reclaim our lives, our selves, our hearts and make decisions based on our truth in life. You are looking to trust wisdom in your life and quit following knowledge on the path of "the" life you're supposed to be living.

HOW LONG WILL IT TAKE FOR ME TO GET NAKED?

This is not a self-help book. This is a self-look book, a picture book actually. We're trying to draw a picture of the true you, naked, not airbrushed. I know airbrushed, believe you me. I can't just "help" you, and if you could help yourself with just a book you wouldn't need this one. You have to really look at yourself naked, think about your naked self, get to know your real authentic self, your likes and dislikes and then you can decide what you might like to change about yourself and your life. It has to be your choice, your plan, your program. Let's be honest, we always want a shortcut. We look for the cookie cutter solution to "make me happy," "make me skinny," "make me rich", but cookie cutter obviously doesn't work very well, or we'd all be happy, skinny and rich. The only thing you have any control over in this entire world is your thoughts, words and actions. This picture book is going to empower you to make honest choices. It's going to finally free up that time and energy you have been searching for endlessly for years. It's going to move you from wishing about things to dreaming about things, because we can make dreams come true.

This is the naked life you've been looking for since you were about 5 years old. Ok, I know you, I know how easy it's going to be to skip through this book and look for the immediate "quick answers." I've done it too many times myself! THERE IS NO QUICK ANSWER SECTION, so quit looking now. Getting naked is not something you want to do real quick and you're going to find out why. Get a pen and some paper, and use it! Actually reflect on the exercises, write on the book, write on the margins, you're going to keep this book forever, don't worry about someone else seeing your information.

Ok, naked moment here. I know you're not really going to write much in this book. You're afraid someone will read it and you'll die an incredibly slow and painful death for being cruel, mean, ugly and honest. We have dozens of books that have very cute "journal" sections at the end of the chapters for you to answer questions and write your honest thoughts, bah ha ha, you never do more than the first chapter, do you? If something is worth contemplation, you should write about it in your own journal. Get a spiral notebook and a writing utensil of your choice, and just write, naked. Write how you feel, make it ugly, juicy, sweet, no editing, no grading, it's just purging. Try it, write something you are quite sure will cause lightening to strike immediately such as "I am soo pisssed off at God!" and see what happens. I'm going to leave you some questions for reflection and contemplation, naked notes, if you will. Hopefully you will use them as a starting place for some "AHAA" moments, maybe you'll write, maybe not, but at least take a few minutes for reflection.

Remember that reflection is pure, honest thought. If you can't be honest in your own head first, it will be very difficult to do it any place else. That's where naked starts. Your friends can buy their own books, this is yours and you don't have to share! We're looking to change your life, not give you more information that won't be used. We're looking for permanent nudity, not a peep show. I suspect you've done too many peep shows with all those other books sitting dusty on your shelves.

GETTING NAKED IS A JOURNEY AND LIVING NAKED IS A LIFE LONG PROCESS

We'll start with your naked story. How comfortable are you naked? We'll talk about the journey to getting naked, we'll talk about creating your naked life and you'll be lucky enough to read several random naked stories, my own and others. All of these things will empower you to get and stay naked. This book is honest and funny, just like you should be. Don't take it too seriously, just roll with the flow. It takes courage to expose yourself, to move through the uncomfortable stages and the painful revelations, but what you will begin to feel is free.

Freedom is something most of us don't realize that we are missing in our lives. We slowly build lives that are based on expectations set by family, associates, media, even ourselves. We compromise our wants and needs very slowly based on what we think our responsibilities should be, and slowly cover our true selves up and slowly lose ourselves. Getting naked is finding your true self again, uncovering your pieces and parts, making authentic choices and moving into your true life. It does sound so simple, "just be honest," but it's not that easy. I know you will be comfortable naked sooner than you think, and it will change your life. Are you ready to move into your real life?

NOW WHAT?

Your first step is to truly make a commitment to change your life permanently, to get to a naked space where you have freedom. You have freedom from expectations, yours and theirs. You live a life that is honest in your thoughts, actions and words. You no longer spend countless hours and loads of energy trying to think of what you will say to people because you are afraid to just tell the truth and let them know how you really feel. What will you do with that time you've been looking for all these years? You will make conscious choices that will help all your dreams come true, of course, and live the life you were born to live. You will finally find and live your own purpose, not someone else's.

I challenge you to commit to being part of the Naked Movement. Become part of a group of people committed to being honest in thoughts, actions and words. Sounds simple, huh? It is, but starting out is not that easy. I want to help you with this journey. I want you to have a safe place to lay those burdens down once and for all. I want you to learn from the lessons I have learned. I want you to be able to breathe and to just be. I want you to get to know one girl, four steps and ten lessons that can change your life forever.

🔊 Freedom. What does this word mean to you?

🔊 Looking back at several situations, I get puzzled at why I continued doing things and then got resentful about doing them. I made the choice to do them. Are there things you are currently doing that you just do not want to do? Name three things you would quit doing tomorrow if there were no negative consequences.

🔊 Knowledge vs. Wisdom, can you hear the difference in your head? Think of it as facts and feelings. Knowledge says what the facts are, and wisdom is what your gut says. How often do you go with your gut? How often do you wish you had gone with your gut?

🔊 Do you think being honest will be worth it?

🔊 Who are you most afraid to tell the truth to?

ONE GIRL: THE NAKED EXECUTIVE

What's a nice girl like me doing in a place like this? Talking about getting naked, exposing yourself, it's all a little "dirty" sounding isn't it?

As you might suspect, this isn't the easy kind of naked, the kind where your clothes come off, burn off, or fall off. This is the kind of naked where you wiggle, you squirm and you are painfully uncomfortable. You take a very deep breath and then you open your mouth and you tell the truth to anyone, at anytime, about anything. Are you sweating or hyperventilating at the mere thought? So why on earth would you want to do that? Well, being naked is the answer to all of your problems and dilemmas. Naked is what you've been longing for and searching for your entire life.

My life is not one of fairy tales or one with a white picket fence house. The oldest of three siblings, divorced parents at age twelve, and a six year time period that looks a little like "Uncle Toad's Wild Ride" at Disneyworld.

My parents were young when they divorced, in their early thirties, in the Kramer vs. Kramer age of divorce when everyone decided to get one. Married young and in the military, they became uncomfortable in the minutea of a normal "post-military" family-function filled life.

I remember the house we rented when we got out of the military and moved back to the "home base" of Tennessee when I was in the third grade. It was an old yellow farmhouse. There was little insulation and no central heat or air. In the winter it was so cold we hung blankets in the doorways and used stack heaters in each room. You might not even know what a stacker heater is, but they run on 220 outlets, with big insulated cords. They have 3 stacks or 4 depending on how much heat they put out. They have a black knob on the bottom of the front and they creak as they heat up the air around them. I can remember that sound in the silence of the night as a child and later as I lay in bed at my grandmother's house when I was in high school.

We rode the bus home from school to my grandparents house in the afternoon where my grandmother was getting home from her job at the knitting mill and my grandfather was waking up to eat dinner and go to his night shift job at K-mart. The treat of the day was having a coke or a sprite after school, a real one in the glass bottles. It was ice cold out of the fridge and we replaced the one we drank with one from the back porch where they were stored in wooden crates straight from the local diner where my grandfather bought them weekly and took the empty's back for replacements.

There were a lot of things that I was naïve about in the third grade. I had lived in Alaska and then Georgia and had been in a sheltered military community of equals, so the concept of fitting in was new to me when we moved to Knoxville. A rather rotund young girl hitting puberty at the ripe age of ten, I would soon find my way to acceptance was good grades, good behavior and exceeding the teacher's expectations. This became the foundation of my behavior from that point forward. It seemed that if I could do these three things, there was always a place for me to fit in.

I suspect I'm like many young women. I learned very quickly how to please people. I learned to keep the peace and to meld into most any situation. I hated conflict and hated being in trouble more than anything in the world. I was one of those kids that rarely got in trouble and just didn't break many rules. I did not want to disappoint people, and I needed them. I needed them to take care of me. I needed shelter, food and security.

The time after my parents' divorce was a turbulent time. My mother's choice of relationship partners fell on the side of passion, which where I'm from means trouble, starting with a former high-school boyfriend currently serving time on drug charges. Of course, I was still naïve, I didn't realize what this world can look like and how quickly things can change. So I went from being a normal seventh grader to a middle schooler who was home alone, trying to make sure her siblings were taken care of, scrounging up lunch money and hoping we could make it through the week. We really didn't have very much food in the house. Mom was struggling to work, take care of herself and be in a relationship with the romantic alcoholic who was loving, caring and hardworking, when he wasn't drinking. Our water was turned off sometimes for non-payment. We figured out how to turn it back on with a tool someone in the neighborhood had. We didn't have a home phone for an entire summer because we couldn't pay the bill. There is not much security for children living this lifestyle. Again, I relied on a proven formula, good grades, good behavior, exceed teacher's expectations. I had some great teachers who really took an interest in me and believed in me. If they had not, I could have so easily taken such a different path with my life. My brother and sister chose to deal with their fear and insecurity in different ways.

My brother, the middle child, and still the most caring of the three of us, followed the drug and alcohol route for relief. At one point in his life, we didn't hear from him for over 3 years. Today, he is clean and sober after battling it out (he decided he wanted to live). He chose freedom. He will tell you this story of why there is no such thing as trash and he picks up everything he can from the side of the road that people are throwing away. Today I know love, and I love him.

My sister, the baby, is still the most sensitive of the three of us. You could look at her sideways and she would cry. She wanted a family. She married and became a mom at 18. She was a stay at home mom until she found herself 80 pounds overweight and miserable with herself and her life. She eventually chose freedom as well, having the courage to leave an unhealthy relationship, live in a tiny home, making minimum wage and collecting food stamps. She inspires people everyday working at a local gym, were she is known for her bubbly personality and her never quit attitude. I will never forget the day she got so mad at me in the hospital cafeteria (while we were waiting for my mom to come out of by-pass surgery) for telling her that "making love to a box of pop tarts after eating an entire dinner was not going to make her pain go away." I made her cry, again.

At the end of my eighth grade year, my mother was a horrible victim of abuse, suffering physical pain and mental anguish at a level I will never know. All three of us were home when it happened. I'm not sure I can remember all the details of that night, but I knew this was not the life that I thought I was going lead. This was not the life I read about teenagers having or saw on television. What had gone wrong in the universe? Why was this happening to me?

After this incident, my mom lost our house to foreclosure. She moved into an apartment and we moved into separate locations. My sister and I moved in with my aunt and uncle. My brother moved in with my dad. The last time I lived with my siblings and my mother or father was when I was 13 years old. My sister stayed with my aunt and uncle for one year and then moved in with my father.

My aunt and uncle became my anchor. They treated me exactly like I was their daughter. There was no need I had that was not met, physically or financially. I got to be a cheerleader, be in national honor society and travel to Europe my junior year in high school. They believed in me and helped me to live. Of course, I was utilizing my life strategy, good grades, good behavior, and exceed everyone's expectations. Yes, I drank some, partied a little, stayed out a little too late with a few people I shouldn't have, but overall, there was very little drama.

My mother continued to lead a more unstable lifestyle. When I was 16, my step-father (the alcoholic my mother had married) was murdered. I remember the Friday night it happened and my aunt and uncle telling me. I came across the back porch, through the sliding glass door with a friend wearing our cheerleader uniforms after a game and they sat solemnly on the couch, waiting for me. I was a little shocked that after all this time, he was finally gone and out of our lives. You see, alcoholics like this never leave your life. Their influence touches everything. I would never be surprised when my mom was seeing him again, even after all of the bad things that had happened. I've learned that passionate love is like that sometimes. Perhaps that's why I have been a little afraid of love my entire life, seeing the types of decisions that some people make in the throes and under the influence of it, tend to make you a little reluctant to jump right in. Once in the throes, it seems people will do anything to get it and to keep it.

Later my mother reunited with another former boyfriend. This one was in the military, he was stable, and promised a normal life. I can certainly understand why she was attracted to that offer. She married and my brother and sister moved with them to South Carolina, where my sister remains living today. I chose to remain living with my aunt and uncle. I wanted to finish my last 2 years of high school where I started and basically didn't want to leave.

I realize this must have been very hard on my mom. Having a twelve year old son now, I can't imagine not living with him again for basically the rest of his life. I would visit them in South Carolina sometimes. It must have felt funny having your daughter be a "visitor." I wasn't very close to my siblings, we just didn't have much in common and had not spent very much time together. I had a holiday relationship with my dad and made sure I touched base and kept in touch with him, but our relationship has always been one of acceptance. Acceptance of who we both are, where we are and what we are able to give to each other. I'm not sure he thinks he has anything to give to me, and in that is freedom as I feel no obligation to make courtesy calls or visits, so anytime we connect, its actually authentic and full of real feelings. My dad is losing his hearing now. He is almost completely deaf and sometimes I wonder if he remembers what my voice really sounds like. I wonder if he remembers what I sounded like when I laughed as a little girl. We never talk about things like that, we never have. I wonder if he thinks about what he missed. As many people my age do, I am watching my parents grow older, watching them suffer the consequences of all of the decisions they have made, the lives they chose to live and I am humbled. How can we ever know if we are making good choices?

College. I remember just following the crowd to complete my applications for The University of Tennessee. I remember wondering how I would pay for it. Would my parents be able to give me any money? I chose to move out of my aunts' house in a rather stupid and unceremonial way, not telling them I was going to until I did, in order to be on my own and qualify for financial aid. I was just moving through the steps of what the crowd was doing next, I certainly didn't have a mentor or a role model that was giving me life advice.

My decision to major in English Literature was made during the middle of my sophomore year. I overheard a conversation between two students about their majors. One guy was majoring in English and the other guy was so impressed because English was so hard. I thought, I've always done well in English and I hate these business classes, sounds good to me. I will major in English. I can always go to law school with that degree.

Truth is, I had no idea was I was going to do. I just needed to get a degree and get a job and make money so that I could be secure and not have to rely on so many people to take care of me, to make sure I had food and shelter. I was always afraid something was going to happen and those things would go away. You see, children do not have the choices that adults do. I will always remember this feeling of total dependence on others. I hated it, mainly because I was let down so many times. I wanted to not have to rely on anyone else. I needed it more than anything else in the world. From the age of 13 on, I had nothing that was really mine. I lived in someone else's house, I relied on the benevolence of others to buy me clothes, to feed me, to buy me a car. At anytime, they could choose to quit, they could conveniently move to another project. This is where real fear comes from. This is where scarcity mentality comes from. You are always afraid that things will disappear and you have no way to replace them. There is no safety net, no parent to rely on, no one to call in case of an emergency. And so you work. You work very hard and you create a fortress. You create a fortress of success. You create a life that looks great on paper. You create a situation where you can buy toilet paper, tampons and deodorant by the cases so you never ever have to worry about running out of them or having to ask an adult to buy them for you because they are not paying enough attention to you to know you need them.

You get good grades, you have good behavior and you exceed everyone's expectations. You become an excellent reader of people, able to adjust your style to theirs, anticipate their wants and their needs and you meet them, and they like you, and you fit in. Then a funny thing starts to happen. You have all the paper products that you need. You have a retirement fund. You have the house, the car, the wedding ring and the toddler and realize, you're still running. You're running to someplace that you suddenly realize doesn't exist.

I have been very fortunate in my career. I went to work for a very entrepreneurial company that allowed people to create their own destiny.

The harder I worked, the more work I got, the more money I made, the more accolades I got. I was on the fast track. I remember dreaming about making 52,000 a year. This seemed like a million dollars. It was 1,000 per week and in my mind I knew when I made that amount of money, I had accomplished something special. I remember the day that happened for me. When I hit that number, it really wasn't enough, because there was more I could make. There were still more shoes I could buy, and I was married and my husband wanted to have a say in everything I spent. This felt an awful lot like scarcity mentality to me. I didn't like it. I tried to cooperate. I tried to collaborate, but it always felt like I had to ask for permission, so I lied. You probably know about these lies. The ones that include shaving off a few 10's or 20's off the price of things, the "it was on sale," the "it was a gift" and of course, you never ever include sales tax in the amount that you paid for it. I chose to lie. I did it to avoid a conversation and a conflict. I assumed one would happen, not that it would have, but I wasn't taking a chance. This was the beginning of sneaking and lying about stupid stuff. The strange thing is, we usually know when we are being lied to. This chronic state of deception creates an environment where you just don't trust each other. The small things become big things, the big things are never discussed in depth and the wall gets bigger and bigger between you. This is true in all of our relationships, personal and professional. I have learned this lesson the hard way.

I currently am a Vice-President of Operations. I was very proud to be the first female VP and the first person outside our founding partners to be a VP. I've made decisions I'm proud of and some that I am not proud of. I have treated people fairly and wish that I had handled some things differently. On any given day, I am compensated way too much for what I do and then the next day I am compensated way too little. I have worked many hours, missed ball games, traveled in tears and drank way too much on the way home after a long trip. I am human. These things are all about my job, about me as an executive. But what about me, the real me?

After my revelation at graduate school about being honest, I decided that I was going to start doing this very carefully in other areas of my life, test the waters, if you will. I decided that I would no longer tell people I was fine when they asked how I was. I decided that when people asked me what was going on, I was going to tell them. I decided to have real conversations and allow others to know the real me and see what happened. Remember, I was already in personal meltdown crisis, so I had nothing to lose.

The March of 2010 evening in Chattanooga started like many others. After a long day of strategic meetings, a small group of professionals loaded up to go to dinner and have a few drinks. This was a small group of 6 folks that I actually really liked. It seemed like a pretty safe place to be honest, if the chance arose. The conversation moved swiftly past the company news and lose ends and quickly to the personal, how are things going, how's your family, what's going on? I knew this was a test. The universe was seeing if I was really going to have the courage. I calmly and a little hesitantly said,

Well, this year is different for me. You know, I have been very blessed with work successes and opportunities through graduate school, but I have realized that fear of failure is keeping me from trying new things and meeting new people. I have decided that whatever it takes,

I am going to let myself suck at things this year. I have given myself permission to be totally terrible. This takes away all the pressure to look good, or be perfect and I can just enjoy trying. I am talking to strangers, taking a trapeze class, a belly dance class, basically things that make me uncomfortable, to see what happens. I know this is a lot of information, but I guess I'm just being naked with you guys. Trying to let you know what I'm really doing.

Everyone looked at me sideways and then our CTO said, "that's awesome. I think it's great." Our HR director then said, "you're a girl looking for real love and real adventure, one naked conversation at a time." Then someone said, "You are The Naked Executive" and that's how one girl started a movement.

That evening, we secured the website to do a blog on living a naked life. At the time, I had no idea that the naked lessons would be so important and that the key to naked was to learn to tell the truth. I found out that to get naked, you have to take on the lies, one at a time. The foundation of naked is honesty.

You can tell the truth, you just have to learn how to do it with compassion and clarity. As the naked executive, I realized people don't tell you the truth because they don't want to deal with your reaction to it. You are causing people to lie to you. If you want people to be honest with you, be honest with them. If you want them to always tell you the truth, make it easy for them to tell it. Learn to get naked and tell the truth, one AHAA moment at a time.

CHAPTER 3

FOUR STEPS: HOW TO GET NAKED

GETTING NAKED, ONE AHAA MOMENT AT A TIME

I've found that the formula to getting naked is simple. It involves four critical steps that must be fully explored. When you are getting naked, you can't go half way, you can't get half naked. The first two steps include identifying your truth and handling the emotions involved. The last two steps involve communicating with clarity and compassion and then accepting the new situation. The first two steps are inside jobs and the last two are outside jobs. The process of getting naked is always the same. The timing may be different, the words a little different, but the process is the same, 1 AHAA at a time.

STEP 1: ACKNOWLEDGE THE TRUTH ABOUT HOW YOU FEEL

Acknowledge who you are and where you are fully, what is the truth?

How this looks in real life

I remember lying in bed trying really hard not to admit that I was really pissed at God. It was not politically correct, it was not Pollyanna, it was not right or ok on a million levels, so I fought it, stuffed it and tried to pretend that I didn't feel that way. It didn't go away because I tried to ignore it completely. As a matter of fact, it just grew and festered, because then I was pissed that there were a bunch of rules I had to believe that didn't let me be mad at God.

How I did it

I was writing in my journal one morning. I was writing about how I felt, where I was, what I wanted, and all of a sudden it just jumped out and onto the page. "I am angry." This was shocking news to me. Angry people do not look or act like me, angry people are not nice and they yell at people a lot. I do not yell at people and I am always polite. This felt pretty good, so I kept on writing, "I am angry that I feel trapped." Hmm, I am feeling trapped, and I am angry, whose fault is it that I am trapped and feel I can't get a divorce....ding ding ding, it's God's! I am angry at God for not letting me get a divorce.

In my journal, I could take off the sugar coating. There was no one here to impress. Why was I continuing to hide myself from the truth? Why in the world could I not admit to myself how I felt? By acknowledging how I felt, I could ask all of these other questions and start the process of change. I could actually feel and then make a choice to do something. But by not allowing myself to admit the truth, I was stuck in purgatory, going nowhere.

When you honestly seek to understand, you will be surprised at the understanding that you may suddenly get. When you carry resentment and anger around it continually sends a message to your consciousness that there are pieces and parts of you that are bad and if people find them out they will not LIKE you (and don't try to act like you don't care if people like you or not). Carrying these things around makes you feel ashamed in the worst way, because you don't know what it is you are ashamed of, you just feel like a big secret keeper. You are not at peace and you feel a constant nagging deep inside you to resolve something that you can't quite put your finger on. Step One: Acknowledge the truth about how you feel.

STEP 2: HANDLE THE EMOTIONS

Handle the emotions, yours and theirs.

Ok, this may not be comfortable. You may truly want to puke and you might come very close to hyperventilating. Stay the naked course and be honest with yourself. Keep the truth in front of you. Yes, your mother may never speak to you again, but that is highly unlikely. Yes, your spouse may lose their temper, but it probably won't last forever. Yes, your best friend may become your ex-best friend, but that may be the best thing that ever happened to you. Don't try to pretend that these things might not happen, that is not reality.

Naked stays acutely aware of what has happened in the past and what might happen in the future and realizes that there is NO way we can know what might actually happen this time. Everything we "think" might happen is actually speculation at best.

How this looks in real life

Once I admitted how I really felt, that I was angry with God for not letting me do something (which upon deeper reflection was really about how he was actually keeping me from being happy because he wouldn't let me get a divorce) I knew I needed to handle the emotions. There are very few things that are more emotional than handling organized religious doctrine. I had to handle the possible consequences of any decision or action I chose. Was God going to be mad at me because I was pissed? What God going to withhold his blessings because I was mad? Was God going to strike me dead? Or worse, I might have bad hair days for the rest of my life? I had to work through the emotions first, then deal with the facts.

How I did it

After thorough analysis of all the possible consequences, I felt I had no choice but to tell God outright exactly how I felt. I was taught that he was loving and that he was benevolent, and I had a very clear understanding of what grace was, so I decided to tell him exactly how I felt, it was time to remove this obstacle and move on with my life.

So I got on my knees and moved to step 3 of the process.

STEP 3: APOLOGIZE UP FRONT

Apologize up front, not for telling the truth, but for the discomfort that the truth might bring to others.

This is a critical step for preparing the relationship for a revelation of truth. If you are going to tell someone something that you believe may upset them, anger them or hurt them, apologize to them upfront for "possibly" upsetting them, but emphasize that you are learning to build authentic relationships and the process involves being honest, then be honest with them. Remember, getting naked is about how you feel. Getting naked is not about telling another person anything about them, that would be a bitching at someone session for things you have absolutely no control over. Getting naked is revealing how *you* feel to someone. Remember, we are always responsible for how we choose to feel. Let the other party know that you are sorry, then forgive yourself immediately for the abuse and disuse of yourself and others. It's really ok, your true self is like that puppy waiting patiently to lick your face even when you've been gone two days. There's no statute of limitations on love here.

We are so incredibly hard on ourselves. We replay messages in our heads over and over, the "I should haves, I could haves." Stop those messages now. They are designed by Mr. Know it All, Knowledge, and there really is no useful purpose for them at all. Get in the habit of doing this in your heart. There are absolutely going to be things you wish you hadn't said or done. Ok, so what? Recognize it and move on.

How this looks in real life

I planned my talk with God like I would a talk with a business associate. I decided that I needed to present him with all the information on how I was feeling. I wanted to let him know up front that I didn't want to be out of the fold, I just wanted a little deeper insight and a little more information.

How I did it

I sat down to talk to God one morning. I shut my eyes and just laid it on the line, but I had to start with the apology first. God, I am sorry I have been hiding from you. You cannot speak to me if I am hiding from you, so I haven't allowed you to work in my life. I am sorry that I have not been honest with you about how I have been feeling, I was scared. But today, I am trusting what you have told us. Today I am trusting that if I am honest and tell you how I feel, you will have answers. I then told him exactly how I felt. I told him I was angry, I was resentful and I didn't understand what was going on in my life. I had always tried to do the right things, be a good person, why was I trapped? Why was I not happy? Why was he keeping me from being happy? I poured out exactly how I felt, with clarity and compassion. I truly was seeking more insight from God, I asked him to just let me know what I need to do, I am willing to do whatever, I have exhausted my resources.

He did answer me, very directly.

Dear Kelly, quit blaming me for decisions that you keep making. God.

After this truthful answer, I was definitely ready to move to the next step.

Step Three: Apologize, to pave the way for the truth.

STEP 4: ACCEPT THE CHANGE IN THE RELATIONSHIP

Accept the change in the relationship. It may be the best thing that ever happened to you.

You may get divorced or you might turn a corner in your relationship and create the intimacy that you've always wanted. You may lose a friend, you may have a relative choose to not talk to you but talk all the time about you. And, this is bad because? You are not satisfied with the way most of your relationships are right now because you are not free to express yourself. You are not living consciously and revealing your true self because you are afraid of people's actions and reactions. When you begin re-aligning these relationships, you will free up energy to actually "do" things instead of thinking about what you have to do or are expected by others to do. You can just live, and that's freedom.

How this looks in real life

People change, relationships change, everything changes. The harder you try to keep things the same, the more they will change. In order to get something different, you have to do something different. You must be ready to do things differently.

How I did it

Once I purged how I felt, I realized that since I didn't think I could be honest with God, I was taking this anger and resentment out on others around me. I was just a little angry. I would get impatient with people that needed me. I helped people when it was convenient, but I just didn't think I could spare any of the stored up "good mood" juice that I had to work so hard to generate. Once I purged, I realized that leaving all of those toxic emotions on a yoga mat or a prayer blanket was a great way of cleansing, of making room for more positive energy and love that I could give to others. I look at time of meditation and prayer as a drop off point for the dirty laundry, a place where I can pick up some clean stuff and tune myself for the day. I accepted that it was ok to be brutally honest with God and I moved on.

STEP FIVE: ACCEPT AND MOVE ON!

This is a pretty basic example of getting naked. I have run through this entire process time and time again. It is very effective when you are giving someone tough news at work, when you are giving a friend fashion advice or even explaining to your child why he is still grounded.

The process of getting naked sounds simple, huh, AHAA. It does sound simple, but it's not always easy. You're going to run into some obstacles, speed bumps, roadblocks and full-fledged construction zones. Be aware.

NAKED OBSTACLES

Naked obstacles will be scattered all along our path. They may be in the form of a speed bump, roadblock or full-fledged construction zone.

A. **Speed bumps**. These obstacles will temporarily slow you down. They make you stop a moment and recommit to being who you are. They may seem small, but small things done on a regular basis lead to big results. They might include you not laughing at an off color joke when everyone else is. Another great example is turning the other cheek when someone wrongs you. You have a choice in having a reaction versus choosing a response. Naked responds. Numb and Dumb reacts and takes no responsibility for the reaction. When you respond with love and patience, you will be shocked at the responses you get from people. Try it and see.

B. **Roadblocks**. Ok, detour ahead. This one is going to take a minute or too longer than a speed bump to get over. It's more an inconvenience to the new life you are trying to build, an "AHAA, caught you" kind of moment. It normally has to do with your deepest hot spot, the one that is the most challenging for you. It may be your mother-in-law relationship, it may be the teacher at school. Whatever the situation, respond with intention. Seek to understand before you respond to anything. This one takes longer because you must care enough about yourself to really reflect on why this situation is causing you angst. You will spend more time in step two, three and four on this one. I think you will be surprised at the answer.

C. **Construction Zones**. This is a major construction zone. As you change and become honest you will have many conflicts within yourselves and your previous thoughts, actions and words. It is very easy to drift back into the old ways of responding since most people act that way, "serve and protect," of course. When you hit a naked obstacle you will be going off-road in many situations and getting off the common path. Call it a rut, call it the interstate of life, call it the freaking Disney World monorail, I don't care what you call it, bottom line is you are being honest, which is uncommon and may absolutely cause shockwaves through our most secure relationships. Do not give up on these. Slowly work through the zone with honest love and compassion and see where you get. There is no way around the construction zone, you're working on sustainable change, so it will all be worth it, no matter how long it takes.

Want a construction project this week? Be honest with your parents. This is a big construction zone area for most adults. We grow up wanting to please our parents for many reasons: to get approval, to get appreciation, to get material goods (good Christmas presents). We learn instinctively how to walk and talk to get what we want. OK, we've done that, we're adults now, time to grow up. Now what? Do you each respectfully communicate your thoughts, feelings and words to each other or do you still have a parent/child relationship based on getting something from each other? I believe the word for this might be co-dependent?

This week explain with love, not anger or resentment, acknowledging it feels different to be communicating in this open honest way, apologize for the discomfort they may feel with this new style, and be honest with love and compassion about what you really think and feel. Start small. It's a big step.

How this looks in real life

It's Christmas season and you always go to your parent's house for Christmas Day. Your mom cooks a huge meal and you spend the day there cooking, cleaning up, etc. Your heart doesn't want to do the giant meal and deal with all the chaos. The meal is fattening, the prep and clean up keeps you from playing with the kids and relaxing. You get anxious, frustrated and a little depressed about it all. This is not what the holidays were meant to be. This year you are part of the naked movement, you feel the familiar feelings, so what do you do differently? You're in the construction zone with an ability to either leave things in shambles or perhaps build something new.

Step 1: Acknowledge the truth about how you feel

Ask questions to seek to fully understand. Don't make assumptions.

"Mom, I know we have always done this Christmas meal each year. Tell me a little bit about what it means to you? How does it make you feel every year?

"Well, its Christmas, I've got to cook, your father loves to have turkey, carve it, put out with all the special dishes, etc. It's what we do."

"Well you know, its so much work the way we've done it, I was just thinking we might look at something different this year."

"Your dad won't like that and for me, I don't know want him upset. Why do you always want to complain about what we do?" Notice this is pretty defensive and this is when your reaction determines the outcome.

"Why do you think he will be upset?" (Notice how you chose to ignore the person zinger she gave you earlier trying to change the subject and make this a personal argument.)

"He likes things the way they have always been."

"Mom, what do you like?"

"What do you mean?"

"Well, it's a lot of work and you don't get to relax or play with the kids. How do you feel at the end of the day?" (Notice the tone and intent of this is to have compassion for your mom, not just get your way and have a change of plans. It makes a difference in how she responds and the general outcome of the conversation.)

"Well, I'm exhausted. I can barely remember the day. I don't sit down. "half of the food gets eaten and the rest thrown away." You and the kids end up yelling at each other by mid-day and it just gets crazy."

"Mom, I love you and dad. I really want to slow things down and connect in real ways with others. I was thinking we could do something different for Christmas that allows us to do that."

Apologize, prior to your revelation

"Mom, I've gotten so caught up in what we should do for Christmas presents, gifts, parties that I haven't really opened up and reached out to others just to see what they have going on. I'm sorry. I get so wrapped up in myself and didn't think about how exhausting and unappreciated you've felt all these years doing all of this work. I wish we had talked about this earlier. Why didn't you say something sooner?"

"I didn't want to say anything about it, I thought if you got mad it would give you the excuse you needed to not come to the house at all."

Accept the change in the relationship

Your mom may not know what to say. She may not trust your intentions. Love her anyway and keep on being naked with her.

Eventually she will realize you are different, you're not just acting different. My mom did.

This is an excellent example of leaning on a "ritual" because we don't trust "love." We don't trust that others will want to spend time with us unless we are doing something for them. Again, fear creeps into our relationships at this point and we become zombies. See how easy it is to become mindless and numb, the opposite of naked.

Parents are tough places to get naked. But, it may give you the most return in all your relationships. Our fears and feelings are reflections, temporary illusions based on stories from the past or predictions of the future. Fears and feelings cannot take away true love for yourself. You may choose to give it away or lock it up completely but it has not gone away. We were given a family with the intention of learning how to love unconditionally, we just mess it up sometimes. In messing it up, we were supposed to learn how to fix it, and that's what most of us are trying to do now, learn how to fix it, finally.

Now you have the basic four-step process broken down. Take a look at it often and practice what it will feel like to be honest with compassion. As you continue on this naked journey, there are several lessons that I have learned that I want you to be familiar with. I want you to be able to recognize the lesson, its importance in your journey and, very importantly, hear the experiences of others.

ↂ In the beginning of my journey I would often write down the entire process as a trial run. I wanted to make sure I was confident in how I felt. I wanted to make sure I had purged all the feelings and emotions I could imagine might come up. I then wrote down how I would feel if someone were telling me the same message (this is practicing compassion and empathy), what would I want the person telling me to feel? Never forget how hard it is for people to tell you the truth.

ↂ Write down a few reactions that you think you might get from friends or co-workers if you began telling them the truth.

ↂ One way to neutralize an uncomfortable situation and give yourself the space and time you need to respond to the situation is to thank the person that is giving you feedback. I use the following statement, "I realize it is very difficult to give people honest feedback and I truly appreciate you taking the time to do this," This doesn't mean I agree with the feedback but it is truthful and keeps the relationship in a neutral situation.

≈ Most people do not make it past the emotional chaos of step 2. They decide it is too complicated and too much trouble to deal with the possible emotional reactions and responses from others. How will you handle the urge to stop at step 2?

CHAPTER 4

LESSON ONE: YOU MUST GET NAKED WITH YOURSELF FIRST

There is only one place to start being honest and it is with yourself. If you think you can get naked by telling other people the truth about themselves, you are completely wrong and this is the wrong book for you. We must first be willing to look at ourselves naked, practice compassion with ourselves first, tell ourselves the truth first, learn how it feels to be told the truth and then slowly and gently begin doing it in our other relationships. There are no shortcuts, you must start with yourself.

Do you know who you really are? Once I heard this little voice in my head say, "how will I know I'm pretty if no one tells me I am?" " How will I know if I'm smart if no one tells me I am?" The answer I heard was shocking, "Who ever told you that you weren't?" It was startling.

Are we what other people tell us we are? If this is true, then are we what the angry road rage crazed driver yelled at us yesterday? It's sometimes shocking that what other people may tell us we are is not accurate or true, but we usually choose to believe it. It's just easy. It's shocking when we realize that there are things our parents have told us that aren't actually true. Oh my God! You're mortified that I would say such a thing about a parent, but hey, it's true. What people tell you are stories, just like the things that you routinely tell yourself.

Can you think of two things that people have told you about yourself that until today you have chosen to believe? Perhaps you have been told routinely that you are not athletic, you are not smart, you are not pretty, do you automatically believe that things? How can they possibly be true?

So if these things aren't who I am, "how do I know who I am?" you ask.

To discover who we truly are we must start by looking at ourselves in the mirror. I suspect many of you have been avoiding all mirrors for a long time, physical ones and mirrors to the soul. Seeing ourselves naked is uncomfortable. It's difficult to quiet the judgmental voice in our head that continually points out all of our perceived imperfections and physical hang-ups.

I bet there are things you don't want to look at when you're naked. We pay all kinds of attention to our "trouble" areas, the ones that don't look like a supermodel's. Turn that judgemental voice off and close your eyes. What does your body look like now? Think about the movement, the muscles, the purpose of each part of your body, how's it doing? There is a purpose for each part and it's not to look pretty, hot or sexy. Which parts are you expecting to be "perfect"? By whose standards? Take a good hard look at your body. Your pieces and parts are your vehicle for this journey. Do you like it? Do you take care of it? Do you want someone else's? What we do for our bodies is a direct reflection of how we feel about ourselves. I know it sucks and I'm sure you don't want to hear about it, but it's true. We don't take care of it because we're not naked. I suspect the more "hidden" your truth is, the more you abuse your body. Now when I say abuse, I mean any form of abuse: overeating, under-eating, poisoning, malnutrition, running it in to the ground with activities, chemicals, stress and responsibilities, lack of positive attention, lack of play and ultimately pure lack of love. It's a machine, unbelievably complex, fearfully mysterious and here to serve you and your purpose. Have you seen James Cameron's Avatar? It's your dragon, one custom made for only you and the only one that you are going to get.

Most of us are not supermodels or professional athletes, but we are all something special. The goal of being naked is to find your true something, to hear your own voice, not all those other voices in the crowd, whether they are cheers or vicious jeers. Find the one voice that matters, it's yours.

YOUR NAKED STORY

To begin the naked journey, you need a true North, a starting place and an ending place. This story must start where you are. I've put together a story starter-a questionnaire of sorts. This is the first step of getting naked, it is the beginning of your naked story. If you do nothing else with this book, please take the time to write the beginning of your story, to see who you are today so you can love the person that you are now and the person you will become.

Copy the following starter sentence and then just answer the questions in your journal. You know, the journal that I told you to get at the beginning of the book since I was certain you wouldn't stop and write in this book! There are no right or wrong answers. There is no need for punctuation, grammar checks or editing. Just give yourself the freedom and the time to be honest, to get naked with yourself for perhaps the first time.

In the beginning there was a (girl, woman, boy, man, frog, dog, whatever you feel safe starting this journey out as) _____. This girl was _____.

This girl found herself in a strange land, one that she knew, but really didn't recognize. Things that had been familiar, now felt foreign. Friends and things that had given her comfort, now had lost their tingle. She was on a quest to discover what had happened, to find out where she was and how she got here. The first thing she did was to look at herself completely and honestly. She looked at her body, her feet, her hands, her face and deep into her eyes and she saw: _____

_____.

When she saw these things, she felt: _____

_____.

And of all the things she felt, _____ was the most surprising. What is this feeling? Is it a familiar feeling or a new feeling? She realized she had long ago stopped her feelings from flowing through her as the pain, disappointment and feelings of helplessness pulled her down into a seemingly bottomless river. She spent so much time and energy trying to stay above the watermark of drowning, fearing with every gasp of breath that this might be the last one she could actually muster up, and she just kept on treading water, in the same place, all the time, over and over again, up and down in the waters of the same place in life.

Suddenly, she was pulled ashore. She was given a towel, a warm towel, to rest comfortably, on a large warm rock, in the sunshine and she was safe to be, and she thought to herself: I have been in this same current for so long, I have long forgotten what it was to be dry, to be safe, to be comfortable.

What is it that I am supposed to do now that I have been pulled from the water?

What makes me happy?

What makes me sad?

When do I feel most alive?

When do I feel most alone?

What do I love to touch, to feel, to taste?

What is pleasure?

Where am I most relaxed?

Who do I talk to that I never have to worry about what I am saying?

If I could let myself feel it, I would feel: _____.

If I let myself, I would: _____.

If I let myself admit it, I am afraid of: _____.

I am: _____.

Take as much time as you can to really begin this journey where you are, naked.

Look at the words you used. How many of them are nouns, adjectives, action words, feelings, and emotions? How surprised are you with your beginning?

If anyone read the beginning of your story (which they won't) would they be surprised? How much are you truly hiding, especially from those who are the closest to you? How much are you hiding from the people in your life that you are supposedly in relationship with, like your parents and spouse?

We hide for many reasons. We usually do this with more good intentions than bad intentions. We might have started to believe at a very young age that the less of a burden we are on others, the more they usually like us. We become master people pleasers, rarely saying no, and often saying yes when we mean no. We avoid discomfort in the name of convenience and avoid conflict in the name of being polite and politically correct. This isn't the way things were supposed to be.

We were made for relationship. Real relationships are messy because we are not perfect people. We have created a world in which perfection is the goal and we all want to pretend that we don't need anyone else. I am not sure how we ever got here, but we are all drowning in that same stream.

I am tired. I am tired of seeing children grow up to be what they think someone else wants them to be. I am tired of seeing families ignore and deny the truths about themselves and each other. I am tired of seeing marriages and relationships fall apart because people could not be honest about how they felt and then love each other through those feelings, whatever the outcome might be. I am just tired, of not being naked. How about you?

So, in your beginning, I want you to slowly get in touch with your naked self and ease into exposing yourself to others. I want you to expose yourself, yes, I said it—EXPOSE yourself. The beginning of getting naked is allowing ourselves to be known so that others will feel empowered to do the same thing. Here is a litmus test, how congruent is the self you are and the self you are showing to the world? If you were on a game show right now, how many people would be able to name 10 things about you that are actually true?

NAKED PEOPLE
MAKE CONSCIOUS CHOICES

A conscious choice is one we make with awareness, and one we take responsibility for. As we slowly become more and more busy and live our lives on auto-pilot, we don't realize how many daily choices we just "make" with no thought or intention. For example:

How do you choose your clothes for the day?

a. I meticulously choose my outfits the night before an event including all accessories, shoes and bag.

b. I match the colors together. Whatever "goes" and is fashionably "acceptable."

c. I choose something that is clean. Outfit? What is that?

d. I choose something that connects to my energy for the day. I pick something reflective and uniquely me. It all just comes together.

There's no right or wrong answer. Please be honest with yourself. It really isn't about fashion.

If you answered a. you are a "Paint by Numbers" person. You are looking for a plan, a map, a template, an example. You just want someone to show you want to do, when to do it and you are certain that you can achieve most anything that is required. As a matter of fact, you seek out people to tell you what to do. You live for the adrenaline of accomplishing what others might think is not possible. You look great, all the time, because you won't go out of the house without being all "put together."

If you answered b. you are a "Stick to the Palette" person. Like the paint swatches at the store, you stick to the palette. There are certain combinations that you like and those are the ones you lean towards. No need to call special attention to yourself, no need to stand out. You like to just blend in. No need to get too creative, wild or crazy.

If you answered c. you are "Clean." There isn't too much thought here on what is layered on the outside, as long as it is clean. Clean is safe, its acceptable, it's never too wrong or too right. It matches anyone that you are with and never stands out in a crowd.

If you answered d. you are an "Artist." You have the ability to just grab something that is stylish, clean and works together. You are not afraid to stand out in a crowd, or to meld in to the background. You see each day as an opportunity to start over and reveal yourself. You rarely wear the same outfits and have a knack for never looking like you have on the same clothes.

How much we reveal of ourselves to others is reflected in our personal appearance. When we are in touch with our authentic selves, we are naked and confident and true in our choices. You are the ultimate piece of artwork, all pieces of yourself, your body language, your spirit and your soul. Hair, clothes, makeup, they should all highlight who you really are, not take away from who you are. Look at yourself right now, what parts of your inside are you reflecting on the outside? Being naked allows these to be aligned.

I find myself becoming more and more inspired by those that dare to look uncommonly beautiful in this world. The people that don't even try to look like anyone but themselves. They know themselves and their appearance is a natural extension of their inner selves. Can you imagine Angelenia Jolie playing Elle Woods in Legally Blonde? It's just not an extension of her self. Are you an Angelenia trying to be an Elle? Are you trying to look "like" someone? What does the real you look like?

This week take a look at a fashion magazine, look at some celebrities, first look at the posed pictures (and yes, they are posed for a reason), then look at the un-posed snapshots catching them in their daily lives. Do they look the same? Obviously the clothes aren't the same, but look at their faces and their body language, read their energy, do they seem content? We have a much keener ability to read people than we think. We don't do it, because we are in a hurry and obsessing about ourselves and what people are thinking of us. Try slowing down and start really feeling people and see how that makes you feel. I have found there are a lot of people out there that would like to get naked, and will, if given a safe place to do it in. You can be that safe place, by letting your walls down and just listening. Be open, be present and be available.

You will feel a physical shift in your energy as you become more open and honest with yourself and others. You will feel a veil being lifted, sometimes veil after veil. You will feel lighter, more authentic, but ironically you will feel safer being in this world.

REFLECTING YOURSELF:
YOUR FAVORITE COLOR

So how do you reflect your personal fabulousness? How do I reflect me? Let's start with a very simple question and answer honestly:

What is your favorite color?

Do not say black. Black is not a color. How does this color make you feel? Do you notice the physical changes in your body as you acknowledge the color and the feeling? That little tingle is your heart and spirit aligning. Stop and bask in that feeling, no matter how small, because you see, its always there waiting for you to acknowledge it and play and laugh about it.

Let's really make friends with your favorite color. What do you own that is that color? When did this become your favorite color? Write a story that includes the color. If your color is blue, does it represent the ocean, the water, a favorite vacation spot? What gives this color meaning in your life? How is this color represented in your life? Are you hiding it deep inside?

Try wearing something, anything, that is your favorite color every day this week (even if it is underwear, you know its there). My favorite color is pink and I have at least 10 pairs of pink underwear. Remember to wear accessories, shoes, a scarf, a purse, jewelry, anything that is your favorite color, on a daily basis. Make sure it reflects your energy and your mood for the day. I realize I am in a funk when I notice that I haven't worn any pink in a while. If I haven't worn it, it means I am probably spending too much time trying to "be" something, to be thinner, to be smarter, to be more professional. I sometimes forget that what I wear doesn't make me any of those things. Pay attention to how you feel and to how others react to you when you are wearing your favorite color. You will be surprised at the attention and comments that you receive.

I see this exercise as a great example of loving ourselves. As small a task as it may seem, it is an exercise in making a conscious choice. One of the reasons that we wander off our path of truth is our tendency to say "yes" when we mean "no." Making a conscious choice about something as small as a color in your wardrobe will build your confidence in making decisions for yourself about yourself. The feeling that you get when you make that conscious choice is called empowerment. It feels the same every time you say "yes" and you mean "yes."

Think about the last time you made a choice that was not aligned. Remember that feeling in your heart and gut? Can you recall the small nagging feeling of obligation and assumed responsibility? Compare that feeling to the openness that you feel when you make a heart-centered decision. The joy that you feel creates an opening in the heart, doesn't it? It's as if you can breathe a little deeper, smile a little longer. Most of us are grownups, and hopefully we don't have someone telling us what to wear anymore. Take the time to do this for a week and see what happens for you. It will build your confidence, open the heart a little and allow for connections to other people. (even strangers, tell them why you are wearing the outfit or piece if they make a comment and see what happens).

AN EXECUTIVE'S WARDROBE

I've been in a traditional job working with physicians for years. I wanted to be successful (duh, no one wants to be a failure) and part of being professional is the attire that we choose. Physicians appreciate a professional appearance. This is a little tricky because you need to be confident, but not arrogant, professional, but not too polished as to make them look unprofessional. Now let me tell you, I've gone through multiple fashion phases and my immediate phase prior to this "official career" was selling Mark Kay Cosmetics! Now, I love Mary Kay, for many reasons. It is a fantastic professional opportunity that truly meets the needs of its customers. I loved the make-up, the energy, the glitter and the prizes. I loved the girlfriends I got to hang out with and lord I loved that big hair and the rhinestone earrings! I still have the star and moon rhinestone set to prove it. It was fun.

When I took my "official" job I realized I needed to be taken a little more seriously in this new position. I went on a nice shopping spree and bought three official suits—real ones. I started along the "professional" path. Now, I still had a little personality, but I was definitely "wearing" the outfit. I still exercised my creativity in the shoe department (as many women do).

Things I learned from this lesson

I dressed to make sure my outside appearance got positive attention. This made me feel smart, which made me work harder, which made me more money, and this was the beginning of the vortex. Sound familiar? I was working non-stop, getting positive feedback and began the process of being a stuffer—a stuffer of real feelings. I couldn't let myself be tired, I wouldn't let myself be sick. I was on autopilot. To stuff the feelings I did very common things, like shop. There were so many kinds of shoes to choose from, and I could afford them! I was so busy, preoccupied, and numb that there was not much hearing wisdom. Wisdom would have been saying "you only have two feet, why are you buying so many shoes?" and "have you noticed that your marriage is a level 2 trauma patient at best, barely breathing, and dying quickly from lack of oxygen?" That's what happens when we get caught up in the vortex. It starts spinning so fast we cannot possibly catch up or think straight.

THE VORTEX

Have you ever watched a cotton candy machine?

When you are in the vortex, you are the stick in the middle, you dip it in the large round metal tub and instantly, before you know it, you're completely covered up and full of hot air, covered in sugar. It's not a pretty picture, and not a sustainable place to be, either. It's so sticky and sweet and melts when anything touches it! But boy that machine can make a giant poof ball around that stick in a hurry.

Unfortunately, it's what we know and it's so incredibly easy to stay comfortably numb in the cotton candy cocoon. That is, until the sun comes out, things get a little warm, and you start melting. Ever seen cotton candy melt? It is an absolute mess! It sticks to everything, even when you try to wipe it off, the stickiness is still there, invisible and annoying. Sometimes it melts layer by layer, and sometimes something happens and it just evaporates—a job loss, a divorce, a broken heart, a death. These events leave us looking and feeling like a toy poodle with a really, really bad haircut. Instant Overexposure!

So if you've ever been instantly exposed, you know what I am talking about. It is like a toothache, that exposed nerve ending that sends shooting pains through your entire body. What really sucks is the way a toothache looks to the outside world. It looks NORMAL, get the picture?

Recognize the signs and avoid the vortex created by decisions making you, instead of you making decisions. Speaking of overexposure, it's very common and it's very important for you to learn about on your naked journey.

OVEREXPOSURE 101: AVOID HYPOTHERMIA

There are a couple of different layers of exposure that you need to recognize and learn to catch early in your naked journey.

Frost Warnings

These are subtle signals and signs that happen in your life that say, "Hey, something's going wrong here. Yellow light, caution, things are not ok." Your relationships may be unhealthy, your eating habits slightly poor, you're in need of an intervention. Hopefully you've felt this nudge, acknowledged it by being naked with yourself (true and honest), exposed the facts and then moved on. Frost warning gone, meltdown avoided. Pay attention to thoughts like, "my relationship is ok, we have fun on vacations and holidays." What about the other 340 days of the year! This is the stage where you can auto-correct with honesty and compassion. It is a danger zone, though, because often times the warnings are so small, it's much easier to ignore them and keep going. But you should know that they never truly go away. Thus the warning: they will come back up at the most inconvenient times, usually in pairs!

Brain Freeze

So you ignored the Frost Warnings and decided to play a little roulette, did you? You felt like you had things under control. You have been pleasantly numb. Then all of the sudden, out of nowhere, ZAP, lightening strikes to the cerebral cortex and you get a brain freeze. A single incident happens that shocks your system. There is no way that you can avoid dealing with this situation. It could be a job loss, no vacation this year, a sickness in the family, child gets arrested. I mean a serious shock to the system. But it is a one-time event. You deal with the isolated situation and crawl back into your numb life. Unfortunately, we never want to look at the core issues that may have contributed to the situation, we only deal with the situation and use the best coping skills we have, hoping. You hope that it will not happen again, and some things don't, but many things do, which leads to hypothermia.

Hypothermia

Ignored the frost warning, did you? You numbed yourself with drinking and no thinking? Maybe shopping and bar hopping? When you are about to hit hypothermia, there is a frantic scurry of activity to attempt to numb it all out. It worked with the frost warning and the brain freeze, but guess what, it won't work now. All of these activities are last minute attempts to stuff down and ignore what you already know in your heart. Something is terribly wrong and it's not going to go away this time.

Your spouse may leave (even if you promise an extra long vacation and to have much more sex!), you may be barely dragging yourself to work each day, or even better, your glamorous job title and salary have been outsourced, along with your dignity and self respect. Oh yeah, your kids hate you too and they let you know as often as possible. Hmm, let's go for the trifecta: get a divorce, lose your job, and the affection of your children at the same time, which does happen to people who ignore the frost warnings. This kind of forced exposure is very painful and incredibly uncomfortable. There's a reason you were trying to avoid it.

Exposure happens and it hurts. At the point of exposure, you fully realize you're not naked and probably haven't been for a long time. You reach a point where you to have to get naked or die and exposure hurts.

Thanks Kelly, this is a great book. What now?

You need to realize I worked very hard to stay clothed for a long time. I've justified, I've vilified, I've testified, I know all the reasons and excuses you can use to say you are not hiding from yourself! You're perfectly fine, you just need a few tweaks here and there. Those hypothermia things could never happen to you, you're too successful, and your marriage can be duct taped together for a little longer. So if this were true, you'd have already made sustainable changes with all those other books you've bought that are on your shelf. I know all about those permanent changes, like the ones you made with your gym membership and your Weight Watchers journal (or 4 or 6 of them) that you have in your purse with lint, gum wrappers and crayon stuck to it. Sustainable change requires something very important, and that is love, real love.

LOVE—THE REAL THING

There are many kinds of love. People think of romantic love and passionate love, but real love is a synonym for compassion. I'll make a very bold statement and bet that you haven't felt much compassion for other people lately. Numb people do not let themselves feel compassion. It requires letting the walls down and actually recognizing what another human being is feeling. All of our energy is being used to serve and protect, so we can't take a chance on catching someone else's bad luck or misfortune. Nope, no compassion or its cousin empathy for us. I hear you now "But hey, I'm a nice person. I'm not mean to people." I understand that, but just because you are polite, does not mean that you are compassionate.

Be honest, you treat everyone with the same "keep them at a distance" politeness that never allows a true, deep connection or interchange. So you're nice. Ok. Is that what you really want to be known for? Is that your purpose, to be nice to people?

Because the word love is so overused, I suggest you perhaps consider thinking of a new word for love. I use the word **true.** It transcends all of the other commonly applied definitions. It is honest, it is pure and something about the sheer simplicity of it sends such a strong message. It just is, no strings attached. So say these words out loud: "My relationship with myself and others is true." What connotation does this have? It's a very strong statement. It's a commitment to naked relationships and honesty in thoughts, actions and words. It has no expectations to be perfect, beautiful or happy. There are no expectations to take out the trash or to have sex every three days. It just is what it is. How much freedom is that? That's the place we're working toward.

Let love, true, in and allow the energy of forgiveness and full exposure to gently melt the walls around your heart, the ones you put there to protect it, to hide your disappointment, to keep that "favorite color" safe because you're afraid that someone will take that away from you too. Let it all go. Fill that space with the light that is love and begin the thawing process. Hug yourself. You're not going to die of hypothermia, you're actually going to be reborn. You get a second chance.

Lesson 1: You must get naked with yourself first, because you must feel safe to get naked with other people, and that is lesson 2.

- Be patient with the process of getting naked with yourself. It may take several months to really get comfortable with who you are, and even then it will constantly change as you learn more about yourself. Each revelation will require emotional energy and reflection. Be patient.

- One of the most useful things you can do is understand being uncomfortable. When you are uncomfortable it is an opportunity to learn something new about yourself. Being naked is being a constant student of yourself. We change all the time. Make a note each time you are uncomfortable. Don't ignore the feeling, ask yourself why you feel that way.

- Change. How do you feel about it? What do you want to change in your life right now?

LESSON 2:
ONLY GET NAKED
IN SAFE PLACES

O
nly get naked in safe places and you know when a place is safe or not.

Do you remember the first time you ever told someone a secret? Do you remember how it felt when they told someone else YOUR secret? That is a feeling we never forget—the first feeling of betrayal. We also remember what it felt like to be told someone else's secret, it felt intoxicating. There was a pure power in knowing you had something someone else did not have. Unfortunately, secrets become currency and we use them when we need more power or prestige. We learn very early in life that there are few, if any, safe places for our secrets.

We've all been there. That unsafe feeling is a huge contributor to why you are where you are today. We read a new book, see a new show, get a little flash of insight, or decide to make a positive change in our life. We get everything ready and run back to our lives, to the same people, places and things. Guess what? They are not naked people! They aren't too happy you're about to make some positive changes. You get shut down, laughed at and mocked, just to name a few. In summary, you get no support.

Remember when a kid in the neighborhood got a new bike, the neighbor got a new car, or better yet, your cousin finally loses that fifty pounds you both have been enamored with for years? Ok, so now what? I believe there's a Bob Dylan lyric for this "come gather round people, wherever you roam... the times, they are a changing..." The familiar "comfort zones" are gone and everyone's "know it all" goes crazy: "Who does she think she is?" "Well, he doesn't need that car, they're so pretentious," blah blah blah. You've heard it all, you've probably spoken parts of it as well and this is another contributor to how we get so shut down. It is no wonder why we get afraid of success. People put you outside that "circle" of acceptable people when you separate yourself from the pack for any reason, good or bad.

There's a warning signal—danger, danger—we're about to lose something here, acceptance, love, perhaps a limb? People want you to get back in line, don't rock the boat, don't be too successful, its makes us feel so bad about ourselves. I've got some big news for you, they are going to feel bad about themselves anyway. They may feel that way forever! You're just an easy target because you actually care about what they think about you and that gives them power.

When you move forward with an open-mind, you will find others that support the naked you. You have to take that chance. You have to talk to strangers when you feel the urge. You need to follow up with a long lost classmate when you have a dream about them. There are people out there right now that will support you, because they recognize you. We're like magnets, and like energy does attract like energy. You'll have people come into your life who support the naked you. You might not want to admit it, but that is happening right now. Look around at what you are attracting into your life. Do you see anyone in your life that you would rather not be like anymore?

Is it true that you can tell a lot about a person by the company they choose to keep? Look around at teenagers, look at business relationships, are your associations healthy, vibrant and growing? Are your relationships a representation of your numbed down dumbed down insides? This is a tough message, but it's true. Let your light shine, the rest takes care of itself. Think about your last vacation. What did it feel like? Were you surrounded by things that you love and love to do or were you trying to just get away from something, anyone or anybody? Just trying to "get away" is another form of self-medicating. You really do just have to come back to your life again.

You do have a choice of who you spend your time with. You can acknowledge these people in your life, the energy suckers. You can be aware and still spend some time with them, they aren't bad people, they are just afraid to be naked. So gently walk into their lives with compassion. As they "mistreat" you, love them anyway. Take their power away by enjoying your life, regardless of how they act. You are well on your way to naked freedom and it will be worth every single uncomfortable minute. You know who you are. You know what can and can't be taken away from you. You have nothing to be afraid of anymore.

TAKE OUT THE TRASH

What do you need to get rid of in your life? What needs to be purged? What is holding old and dead energy that is surrounding you? Do you have room to breathe in your house, your car, your closet, your life? Is stuff crammed everywhere? How reflective is that of your life?

While I was working on this book I kept stumbling into massive roadblocks in creativity, energy, and just plain old "want to." I would schedule time to edit and polish the manuscript and then just not "want to." I would spend hours waffling between the shoulds and "want-tos." I kept looking for a comfortable flow and routine. This time period for me was very transitional. As you know, every part of my life was in a state of new beginnings and now I felt that I was being asked to even give up what I had been clinging to as a solid foundation—my daily routine. As I had these honest thoughts, I realized that perhaps I was clinging to a routine that I didn't need anymore. "But I'll never make myself workout if I don't do it at 5:30 am" and "I can't write and work out at the same time" and "evidentially I can't do anything past 8:30 pm in the evening because I want to go to bed or do anything mindless." But, really, this was just another example of a struggle against change.

I was struggling against what was familiar and something that I thought I could trust. Another word for this is a rut. I have never thought about the difference between a rut and a routine. In thinking about it, I realize there is very little difference. I had to get naked with myself and realize that I was talking and writing about getting naked, living an adventure, letting go and trusting, but I wanted everything to get in an orderly line and wait to get on the roller coaster at a convenient time and place to make the experience as stress-free as possible, ha! See, these things just creep up on you. I have to think it is just walking the naked journey and continually making a commitment to self-awareness and honesty in our own paths. Trust the process, Kelly. Eat when you're hungry, sleep when you're sleepy, rest when you are weary, the rest will take care of itself. Remember, Eve was not worried about how much she weighed or that her hair needed to be highlighted really badly.

❧ Sometimes we stay friends with people out of a sense of obligation or pity. Do you have any of these unhealthy relationships right now that you know are not safe?

❧ Who do you know you cannot trust?

❧ How do you recognize a safe place? What does it feel like?

❧ Do you think safe places exist?

❧ Can other people trust you with their naked information?

CHAPTER 6

LESSON 3: NAKED IS SOMETHING THAT YOU NEED TO EASE IN TO

E
ver jump into an ice-cold swimming pool? Your body temperature gauges let you know real quickly exactly how smart this idea was! Ever get brain-freeze from eating ice cream too fast?

In order to get naked and stay naked you need to ease in to it. If you just decide you're going to rip the band-aid off and start telling everyone the brutal truth without any compassion you will probably get shot! You are getting naked to build relationships, not to destroy them. Telling someone the truth without compassion is cruelty—never forget this lesson. You never have to compromise your message, but you can always change the manner in which you are delivering it.

Let's take baby steps, ease into it a little at a time. Remember your favorite color, that's a baby step to stop a minute and actually think about something that is truly you. Remember the "parent test," being honest with your parents for a week, that's a baby step. A great way to start easing into naked is to actually listen to questions people ask you, and then truthfully answer them. Fair warning: they will be shocked. Some may actually stop asking you questions when they realize you are going to answer truthfully. That's a shocker, most of them didn't really want to know the answer anyway.

The next time someone asked you what you want to do tonight, think a minute, and then just go with what your heart says. Tell them the truth, even (and especially) if it's to not spend time with them! When you're bored and restless, do not give in to the lure of the numbing box—television! This is a recipe for brain drain. There's a place for television as a form of entertainment, but when you are using it to numb your mind when you are bored, you are cheating yourself out of doing something that will help you grow more naked. Watching television is not "doing" something, it's watching other people do things. Think about that for a minute. Watching other people's lives on television can leave you with yet another reason to think about the past or to put something on the list to do in the future. In order to grow, you need to balance your life with doing and being. Where do you think mindless television watching fits in?

Ask yourself the question, "what do I want to do?" Not what should I do, what can I do, what can I make myself do, but "what do I want to do?" Then proceed to make that happen, even if it is a tiny act, like washing your face. Seems a little ridiculous, doesn't it, but what you are doing is training yourself to find your bliss, follow you heart, trust wisdom of the moment.

As you do this with the little things, your mind will be able to hear some of the bigger things, because it trusts that you are going to listen. I promise this is true. Do not fill your life with obligations and responsibilities. This is not a naked life, it is servitude—servitude to a master that doesn't actually exist, you just think it does because it feels safe.

You see, when we take the time, even if it's a short period of time, to acknowledge and nurture our naked self, wisdom grows and knowledge settles down a little. The war between wisdom and knowledge will battle on and rage for a while, but truly acknowledging and loving all of your selves is what naked is all about.

Remember to ease into naked at work as well. Living two separate lives is exhausting. Eventually your body becomes so confused it just doesn't know who it actually is and this can definitely be a contributing factor to being shut down and closed off. You become afraid that people are going to get a glimpse of that other side of you. You spend incredible amounts of energy "pretending" who you are and what you really think. Lord, this is just exhausting. I know. As you ease into naked, you will start making honest comments automatically. Honest comments lead to honest conversations.

At first, people will be very skeptical and non-trusting of your motives and intentions. Don't blame them or react to them. Remember, open up, be naked in your actions and thoughts, not just your words. This process takes time and practice, but it does matter and you will wake up one morning and all of the sudden realize that all your "parts" are starting to align, including your personal and professional selves. You will have so much more energy to do what we're all looking to do—fulfill your purpose and enjoy life.

CAUTION: YOU CAN GROW WEARY GETTING NAKED

Because we are living so much more present and open in the now, it takes more of your active resources. You are letting in "unfiltered" information. Think of it as high fiber cereal. Hmm. Get the visual? You should be aware of what this is going to do to your mind, body and spirit. Your mind and body will fatigue much quicker than your spirit. You can get frustrated and down really easily when you're growing because we are so used to our mind being able to control our bodies. We can push them and push them until they just drop. This process is killing us very slowly (and sometimes not so slowly).

At times I've felt in a purgatory of sorts, I'm naked enough to know I can't go back to being closed off and shut down. I know where I am is uncomfortable but I can't see where I'm going, so I'm in no man's land. At this point, you've left the shores of comfort and familiarity, setting out for a new distant land full of milk and honey, you're excited, you're in the boat, and a huge fog rolls in. You can't see what is in front of you at all and panic can set in very quickly. You know you can't go back, that shore is a distance memory, but you can't see ahead, so what do you do? Well, if you're like me you spend a lot of time at first lamenting why you left the damn shore in the first place. This is when the waffles begin! Ever watched a toddler throw a temper tantrum? That was me in the boat at this point, jumping up and down, stomping my feet, crying a little, but the boat didn't move, it stayed eerily anchored, right where it was. I finally got so tired that I sat down and shut up. You will too when you realize the boat is not going to move. Then you start to notice that the water is kind of calm and you're actually moving somewhere, albeit so slowly that you hadn't even noticed. Then you notice that you're moving and you're not actually paddling the boat. It starts to hit you very slowly that perhaps it's pleasant here—with no drama, no worries, just you in a boat, moving slowly but steadily to whatever is on the other side of the fog. Every once in a while, you might catch a glimpse of what is on the other side. You can see it in your mind's eye and you start to dream about it. The more you let yourself dream about it, the more detailed the dream becomes. You aren't worried about the rights and wrongs of the dream anymore and you just let your heart create anything it might want to, regardless of how wild or far-fetched it might once have been. You realize this is what they mean when they talk about creating a vision. Hmmm, it's much easier than you thought it was going to be. And you spend less and less time thinking about what you left and more and more time "seeing" what is behind the fog. Then one day, when you least expect it, you wake up and you're there. You're on the other side of the fog and it feels just like what's been in your dreams. You realize all you really had to do was leave that other shore and trust that the boat would get you there eventually. The sooner you settled down into the boat, the easier the journey was. Life carries us through the journey if we allow it to, but this can cause us to grow weary. You really need to prepare for the Wearies.

THE WEARIES

Let's define weary so you know the difference between weary and tired or frustrated. Weary is a little bit of a lot of things—a little afraid, a little sad, a little tired, a little angry, a little impatient. You just aren't enough of any one of them to be "something" else. So this is weary, understand? You need some down time, to be naked alone, to get your mojo flowing again, to get your energy charged, and you need to let all of these "littles" flow through you, and then out of you, but NOT stay with you. You need to get grounded, you know, like a lightening rod, and then you can once again contribute to the naked movement.

Remember that we are all energy conductors. Those wearies are little energy pockets that are moving in multiple directions and keeping you in a state of fatigue. Nature is there for us to connect to and to be grounded with. The Wearies have familiar pathways and connections that they have been accustomed to. When you were sad, you ate something. Bye, bye sadness. Once you had eaten, you had shame and guilt to deal with (but sad doesn't care because he's taken care of himself and he gets relief). Now that you're naked, where do those little sad wearies go? They can't go where they used to because you won't let them. You've left that shore for good. Let them go back to where they came from, open up to the energy, connect to a source that gladly holds them freely—wisdom says so.

When you find yourself dealing with the Wearies you might: soak in the bathtub, with Epsom salts and aromatherapy oil such as lavender, and feel those wearies just move right through you and into the warm water and dissolve.

Put your feet on the grass, spread your toes, shut your eyes and feel those wearies run down into the soil, dissolving into the earth.

Lay on the ground and watch the clouds float by. Just lay there, watching the Wearies float out of your body and dissolve into the clouds as they float by.

Light a candle and watch the flame flicker gently. As you sit and watch, let those wearies melt into the flame and as the smoke rises, dissolve those wearies one by one into the flame and then the smoke.

Yoga can help move those wearies out of your system. Listen to your body, where are those wearies hiding? Gently massage them out of your system with breath and movement.

Listen to some soothing music, preferably without words, or better yet words in a foreign language that you don't understand. This allows you to really concentrate on the music and rhythms. Notice how your wearies can move through the rhythm and out of your body when you let them.

Walk. The rhythm and cadence is like wiggling that tooth, eventually it will come out.

You must get rid of the Wearies in order to let energy flow through you, heal you and move you through the fog to your shore. If you don't allow them to flow, it will be a long and rocky ride.

NAKED PARTS NEED SUPPORT

I am a fan of Spanx! But we are not talking about that kind of naked support. Support comes in all different sizes, shapes and colors. Your support for naked parts will be through wisdom.

Wisdom is that feeling that tells you if someplace is safe or not. It tells you whether someone is safe or not. Love your naked self and listen to that voice. You will find yourself opening up to strangers, just because. You will find a whole new world out there to love and support your parts. It's like a giant connect the dot board, everything just falls together at the right time and the dots connect. Remember that I told you you'd be a magnet? Remember what happens when you flip a magnet to the wrong side—polarity, not attraction. That is not what naked is. Create your own situations to build trust in humankind and you will find that most strangers are more open to your naked self than people who know you. Why?

Strangers have no history, there is no ego in your relationships. You haven't screwed things up yet with lies and deceit. We all know when someone is not telling us the truth, we just choose to ignore it because it's convenient and feels better. You can begin a naked relationship with a stranger because it is safe. They sense you are honest and open and respond openly. Most of your current relationships are numb and dumb and very sensitive to change. You will find support and connectedness to the real you that is waiting patiently to play in the big world again. Have fun, enjoy life, let people get to really know you, it really is what life is about.

RELATIONSHIP RE-ENTRY

I want to give you a couple of quick thoughts about re-entry to your current relationships. We've talked a little about our fears of failure and success. Understand that naked is the ultimate success. It is the freedom and the secret that everyone is looking for. Naked is actual contentment with this moment, as it is, without any wishing. People around you will be unsettled. Some people will be jealous, some will be angry, many will feel threatened.

Gay Hendricks has a fantastic book, *The Big Leap*. This book talks about the unconscious fear we have of leaving other people behind when we have positive change and growth. What do you think about this theory? Have these thoughts ever crossed your mind? Who do you worry about leaving behind—a spouse, parents, college friends? Do you think if you quit "behaving" they won't want to be around you anymore? (This is a primal fear we have, other people not liking us, don't deny it!)

Take a deep breath, stop the color commentary and trust that your new friends are out there, waiting to meet you. You just have to show up and be a naked magnet.

○ Sometimes people ask us to tell them the truth and then are mad that we do. Describe a time that telling the truth was just not worth the effort.

○ Talk a little bit about a decision to not tell the truth that you regret today.

○ Does telling the truth sooner or later cause more pain?

LESSON 4: YOU CAN'T MAKE OTHER PEOPLE GET NAKED

Y
ou can't make other people get naked. Yes, it's the ex-smoker dilemma. One you start feeling positive changes in your life and the momentum from being naked, you become the naked poster child. You will want to shout it from the mountaintops, you will want to tell people at the bus stop, "hey, get naked" but naked is something people do on their own timeline. The only thing you can do is be naked and let them see the changes in your life.

Your relationships will start to change because you are changing. You'll want loved ones to change with you, to just throw caution to the wind and do it—rip the band aid off! You'll want to hold a Nakedfest at your house for all your friends, neighbors and co-workers. Sorry, this won't work. People must be willing to walk into the light because it is their light. People will try to temporarily drain energy off of your light source and, like two little lightening bugs, you're great for a short period of time. Very quickly you realize they can't create their own energy, their own light. They become a predator, feeding off of you.

Have you ever had a friend who hears that you've lost weight and they instantly want to be your diet buddy? They want to eat what you're eating, exercise like you're exercising? I think they want to do this because if they don't lose weight like you have, then somehow it's your fault! This is a predator, first class number one. You cannot let this happen. Love yourself, listen to your body and mind. You know when someone is draining you. Quit ignoring it and let them find their own path. You must, it's a rule, you just can't make others get naked, no matter how much you want them to.

Most of us have known an addict of some type, an alcoholic, drug addict, etc. You understand that no amount of "rational" arguments you make will cause them to just "quit" what they are doing. You simply cannot love an alcoholic sober or a drug addict clean. It is impossible to comprehend why this doesn't work or why they make those choices. Remember, they are human just like you are. They have a "know it all" too. Their "know it all" works overtime to convince them of their inability to change their lives. The story goes on and on in their heads, just like yours. It's a battle that many of us will be fortunate enough not to have to deal with.

My brother is an addict. He is now clean and sober, but always an addict. I'll be honest, I don't really know his story. I don't know when he started using, I don't know why. As I type this I realize I have never asked. I know he went to rehab in high school and that was when he lived in South Carolina and I was still living in Tennessee. I wasn't there when they took him to the hospital and dropped him off, I wasn't there when they had family counseling or family visit day. I never spoke to him one time.

I really saw this as "not my problem." I thought he was a pain in the ass. There was so much drama. It reminded me of all the drama with my mom and her abusive alcoholic relationship. I wasn't close to him or my sister and I was not involved in their day-to-day lives. I was living a life of one, by myself, with no close attachments. Self-preservation was my goal. I just wanted to be normal and have a normal life. I realize now that I was too caught up in trying to "make it" somewhere. I was trying to get to that proverbial high ground where things like drug addictions cannot reach you or your family. Like many people, I think unconsciously I thought addicts were selfish and just weren't strong enough to pull it together.

My brother, well, he is the most caring one of all of us. He is the one that always brings my mom a card and a rose on Valentine's Day. My mom loves him differently than she loves my sister and I. She doesn't love him more, just differently. As a mother now of a son, I can empathize with her. I realize that where we see a grown man, she still sees her ten year old little boy. I know other mothers that struggle with this now. I see them cry. They are in so much pain at the torment their children are in. They feel somehow that they contributed to the problem and they feel helpless that they cannot fix it or make it go away. The addict is a tortured soul, afraid of reality and unable to pull out of the cycle by themselves, yet they must do it alone and for themselves only, when they are ready.

The last time my brother was in rehab it stuck. He decided he wanted to live. To my knowledge he's never had a relapse since then. I have watched him work extremely hard to build a real life for himself. He is a cook. He has been in the same job for longer than most people. He never misses work. I watched him get a small apartment that was close to a bus stop so he could ride to work. I have never ridden a bus to work. I watched him work two jobs just to buy food. I have never worked two jobs. I struggled to lose weight always wanting to cheat just a little, he could never cheat just a little and have one little sip of alcohol. He did whatever it took to live a real life. I was still living a fake one, and I knew that people didn't look at us that way. On the outside, I had a life and he didn't. They were wrong. He learned what life was. He learned to appreciate everything, every little thing, regardless of its cost. His favorite cost for things is free.

Joe is a junker. He loves to pick things up off the side of the road. He started this way before recycling and repurposing were cool. He started before there was American Pickers or any other glamorized television show about junkers. If you have something that you want gone from your house, anything, he will take it. He always knows someone or can find someone who needs it. He is always swapping things, selling things, and ironically, fixing things. I have given him more junk that he has fixed or sold than I can imagine. I like it. I love it, actually. He called me last night and told me about the lawnmower that I gave him a while back. It didn't work when I gave it to him, but a guy finally found a small part that he thought he needed and it finally started today. He was so proud to say, "I have a brand new lawnmower." I was amazed. It was a piece of junk in my shed that I just wanted to get rid of. He has a lawnmower.

My brother and I went to the hospital not long ago with my mom as she was having a complete knee replacement performed. He and I were together in the waiting room for several hours. I was going ape-wild and was incredibly uncomfortable as this OR waiting room was full of families that thrived on the hospital experience. You know the ones, they have 14 people that show up because Aunt Bethel is going to have her procedure done today. This is a social opportunity for all family members to catch up on every single detail of everyone's life for the past 10 years. I swear to you, it is a family reunion! They have people calling the pay phone all day long checking on Bethel, 4 preachers come by to check on the entire family and did I mention they have several babies with them that the grandparents are watching and there are 4 people with the same name, all called Granny? They are everywhere in the waiting room. I secretly think they are there for the cheap cafeteria food.

So we're stuck, Joe and I, together, for what would be about 6 hours. He has taken the day off from work, so he is relaxed and thankful to not be working. I never officially take a day off, but I can't get much done from a no cell zone in the hospital, and I am learning to be uncomfortable, and I am! What am I going to do here all day? Ok universe, why am I here today? Who am I supposed to talk to do?

So I started talking to Joe. I leaned into being uncomfortable and tried to seek to understand someone else. I was tired of thinking about myself and where I was and where I was going and what I needed to do all the time. I just started asking him questions and we had a conversation, probably the first one I ever had with him. I actually listened with interest to what he said. I learned a lot about him and even more about me. I started with a very naked question, "Why do you want to pick all that trash up from the side of the road?"

Where I live, there is always something on the side of the road on trash day. People are constantly putting out the stuff they no longer want or need.

Joe likes to think of himself as a treasure hunter. He doesn't see anything as trash. He sees a few extra dollars, a new toy, something broken that just needs a little TLC to be running again. He told me about some lanterns that he found that were antiques that he sold for fifty bucks. He told me about a huge aquarium that he found that he cleaned up and set up in his house. He told me about the things that he swapped out for pieces and parts of things he actually needed. This was all really fun for him. His eyes lit up, he was excited talking about the things he can do with something that costs nothing. It warmed my heart to see him so excited. I thought people only got this excited when they talked about what they did for a living, their new cars, or the vacations they were planning. I laughed so hard with him. He was telling me stories that I had never heard before and was so open about who he was and how he felt about trash and picking it up from people's yards. He gave me a safe place to be naked by being naked himself.

I confessed that I didn't think I had the courage to ever stop my car at someone's curb and pick up something they left for trash, I didn't care what it was. What if they saw me getting it? I can hear his voice right now saying, "Well, I just smile and wave at them. Thank them." Well, that thought never crossed my mind. You see, I was realizing that the world was much bigger and different than I thought.

All of a sudden it hit me; Joe was like a thrown away toy. There were many people that left him on the side of the road when he was using. Most people thought he would never change, never get clean, hold a job, or be a real part of our family. I was one of those people. I didn't think there was anything I could do for him and he didn't care enough about me to do anything for himself. I am ashamed of that time I spent in hiding. Hiding from the "dirtiness" of having an addict for a brother. It just didn't fit into the life I had imagined, so I ignored it completely and Joe, I am extremely sorry.

I wanted to be the family in the magazine, great house, good looking, fantastic vacations, you know the picture in THE magazines! When things happened that didn't fit in with the magazine image, I got mad. Who did I get mad at? Well, the same person we all get mad at, everyone and no one in particular. We just fester about how other people (no defined others of course) screw up our lives. Your life is screwed up because your spouse didn't get the yard cut before the Easter lunch you wanted to prepare for your extended family, your plates don't all match and good grief, none of those things are really important.

I could have learned a lot from Joe. I could have learned humility, grace and gratitude. I could have learned courage and fearlessness, but I thought I knew more than him. I could have learned what joy was and happiness as well. Perhaps I thought I was a little better than him, having a college degree and all. I was wrong. He is a more courageous person than I will ever be.

I'm sorry, but you can't make others get naked. You can't love addicts clean, you can't make your spouse tell you the truth, and you can't make your girlfriend see that she is overweight because she eats junk all the time! People will only get naked on their timeline, in their safe place. What can you do? You can be naked yourself. By allowing others to see our naked selves (as my brother did for me) it allows them to reveal a little bit of their true self. Once you get a small taste of acceptance when you're quite certain you're going to be ostracized or outcast, you build some momentum. You realize that maybe, just maybe, you can tell people the truth, let them know who you are and they will accept you, naked.

୧ Think about a time when you knew someone was in denial, when they were lying to themselves and everyone else. How did you handle the situation? Did you attempt to help them get naked? How did that work out?

୧ Do you have a relationship that you are hiding from others? Are you ashamed or embarrassed by a relative or relationship? Tell me a little about a time when they made you uncomfortable.

୧ What strategy do you use to help others get real with themselves, get naked? Do you confront them, educate them, conjole them? Which strategies have worked for you?

୧ How honest are you with other people about yourself? Name three areas that you are consistently vague about, let's start with how much you weigh.

CHAPTER 8

LESSON 5: EVERYTHING JUST FEELS BETTER NAKED

Have you ever taken a shower with your clothes on? Jumped in a pool with them on? You know that feeling of drowning, of an enormous weight on your shoulders? What if your life right now is that way? What if you're actually waterlogged and you don't know it? If it is what you have always felt, how would you know it's not normal? We're all carrying around baggage, a bag called guilt, a bag called shame, and several others. We're very used to carrying these things around and they are so heavy. We picked them up in the past and think we need them for the future. Unfortunately, we don't stay in the present long enough to realize we can set them down and walk away.

When you're not naked, you aren't living in the present, you are always some place else. We're dwelling and reflecting on the past looking for patterns and trying to learn something to help us or protect us. We're ashamed of something we did, we beat ourselves up constantly, and we're not free. If the past is not where you like to hang out, then you're probably looking toward the future. No matter what you're looking at, it's because things are either going to get better or things are going to get worse and it's the same burden and the same amount of energy utilized.

When I was married my husband and I both lived someplace else. We had totally different time zones and zip codes. I lived in the future because I was hopelessly optimistic, and I refused to slow down and acknowledge the moments in the present that contained conflict. I had a great pain-avoiding sensor! I would numbly and with a smile "cheerlead" myself to the next day. My spouse was the opposite. He had moved a long way from his family and missed them deeply. He often reminisced about them and his home. He might have been afraid that the future would not have been as good as the feelings he recalled from the past. We were both afraid.

Now this causes an interesting dilemma. Neither of us was present. Neither of us had the toolkit to deal with our own pain, much less support each other to grow and heal. We both made huge assumptions and acted/reacted accordingly. He felt I was a master conflict avoider and I felt he was a melancholy family boy who would never let anyone but his family have a chance to be in his life and to be happy. So we numbed things down for 16 years, until it was too late to thaw things out and fix them, unfortunately, there were no take back allowed.

I did get naked with him eventually, and he's grown much more naked as well. I told him I was truly sorry for being the ice queen. I was sorry I couldn't say how I felt; I just didn't know how and couldn't get there from here. That's why I'm here now. I sincerely hope that you can commit to getting naked before it's too late. Learn to communicate honestly with compassion, learn to forgive, learn what true is and make the world a less cold and covered up place.

When you're MIA, you totally lose time. You look through photographs and see snapshots in time you really can't remember. You see your child grow up in pictures because you can't remember the day in your mind or the memories of that day are of the negative thoughts and feelings and anxieties. You remember you had a really bad hair day and felt fat, instead of remembering the way your child's laugh sounded at his three year old birthday party.

Time stops for no one. Nor does it go backwards, ever. This moment is now and the only real thing that we have. So, as you wake up from your long winter's nap, here are a few things to take note of. Notice how they sound, feel and smell. Make this memory part of your wisdom—beautiful, not judgmental and lacking. Every moment is just as it was meant to be, full and complete, not good or bad, or lacking in any way whatsoever.

Children, parents, animals, planets, all have lifecycles. Be an observer of them, with all your senses, be attentive. Listen; trust that by putting your "know it all" wants aside you can open up to feeling through others. "Where two or more of you are gathered in my name," when two or more connect on an authentic level, you exchange energy and the experience is multiplied and that positive experience is multiplied and that positive experience is projected out into the universe for others to grow on and from, and feel and see, and you have made the world a better place by being naked and present. This feels much better than cold and numb and very alone.

Naked pain feels "better" as well. When you are naked you know and fully accept that everything changes, therefore, pain is a feeling and only a visitor to be handled the same way. Acknowledge, handle the emotions, apologize, and then accept where you are, grow and move on.

Pain either moves through you or gets stuck in you. It's always your choice. You can help pain flow through you by not resisting, not struggling against it. Yoga teaches us to relax, to be aware of struggle and seek to release it.

Although Yoga seems to be the newest fitness craze, it's actually ancient in its principles. It is an excellent part of a naked environment. It gets your mind in touch with your body and helps you see the actions and reactions of each. It calms the mind, allowing the body to respond (think Dragon in Avatar). Harness the energy and use it for building your own naked environment. You'll be amazed at what you can actually accomplish when you start working with your parts instead of against them.

CHILDREN NATURALLY PRACTICE COMPASSION AND THEY ARE NAKED

We come into this world naked as children.

When we were children, there were no titles, no genders and no labels. Remember when there weren't boys and girls, you just had friends? We didn't have these labels until kindergarten and they had to have a way to divide everyone up to go the bathroom. Remember when you played together and had no worries and you didn't know what rich and poor were? I suspect many of us didn't. Where are those friends now?

I think as children we have x-ray vision. Children can see the soul before anything else. Children rely on wisdom because they haven't been granted the "gift" of knowledge. They see love before they see fear, where knowledge tells adults that sometimes love hurts, so beware. Children see light, they love and they play. Their wisdom senses when another child is hungry and they share their lunch or snacks (our knowledge says, don't share, you might get hungry later). Wisdom sensed sadness and asked the person who was sad what was wrong. We genuinely wanted our friends to be happy, so we could play together, right? Are you starting to see how knowledge is clouding up your ability to hear wisdom? Are you starting to see how knowledge is influencing your ability to trust, to reach out to others, to have compassion? Knowledge looks at the past and recalls all the bad and looks to the future with fear of the past repeating itself.

When knowledge entered our world we began to recognize time as the past, present and future. We learned what it felt like to lose something, which created fear. Perhaps this ancient pain lies deeps within all of us. I suppose this type of pain is the loss of connection that Adam and Eve might have felt. When we feel something similar, we react and bolt and do whatever necessary to do what they did to "cover up." Are you starting to get the big picture of how you got so "covered up" and why it is so hard for us to set this baggage down?

This is not how we were supposed to live. We cannot actually be fatally wounded with knowledge. We have wisdom as protection around our hearts We're just afraid to trust that it is thick enough to keep us from dying of heartbreak. Everything feels better naked, because that's what freedom feels like. No guilt, no regret, no shame, only freedom.

⌖ If you had no worries or concerns, what would you do today? What about tomorrow?

⌖ When do you feel guilty? Do you remember the first time you ever felt guilt? Where did it come from?

⌖ What is your biggest fear?

CHAPTER 9

LESSON 6: STAY AWAKE AND AWARE WHILE YOU'RE GETTING NAKED

GETTING NAKED WHEN YOU ARE DRUNK DOES NOT COUNT

N o, it is not courage in a bottle! Getting naked leads to a path of acceptance, respect and love for your self and others, to a compassionate and true connectedness for our "commonness" at the human level. SO, getting naked when you are drunk does not count! After getting naked you should feel lighter for the journey, more connected to your self and have no regrets. You should be more energized, wanting to share the journey—no hangovers, no sleepovers and no regrets. I can feel you getting flustered up. I know you've had those great nights of "splendor in the grass," moments of rock star, flashes of insight, and perhaps more than one incident of instant exposure that led to naked bliss. I KNOW these things. Sorry, they just don't count. There's a two drink limit. Anything after two, you're on your own.

Getting naked is supposed to make the road a little lighter, to remove a layer, to get connected to the self and recognize wisdom. Drunk is numb. I don't care what you say or think, I'm talking about a no-fly zone after two drinks! You may think that alcohol is courage in a bottle, but its actually cowardice in a jug. You just can't be honest in your thoughts, actions and words if you can't walk straight, feel your nose, and if you're slurring your speech. Now don't get me wrong. I enjoy adult libations, but be honest, they always have a tailwind that contributes negatively in some way to the fabulous life that you are trying to build for yourself.

Physically, it alters your metabolism, your energy levels, your sleep habits. Don't fib to yourself, you know it does! Not to mention those empty calories that it packs on your butt. Now, if you enjoy the way it tastes, great, just don't overindulge. If you are honest and you're drinking to ease stress to relieve your pain or generally to make yourself have a good time, this is a huge indication of at least level 2 brain freeze stage, if not full hypothermia! Stop and look at your life. Are you attached to that feeling? What is the feeling you're trying to get to? How do you feel the next day? Did you play "phone a friend" or "find a friend"? What about the sugar crash the next day? Really, it just sling shots you back to reality and deeper into the dark cocoon. And let's face it, it is so unattractive to cry your eyes out when you are drunk!

Let's take a quick timed test. You have 1 minute to answer each of the questions below: Write as many things as you can in 1 minute:

1. List your favorite alcoholic beverages.
2. List your favorite things to do, your hobbies.
3. List things you do for fun and to relieve stress.
4. List what you did last night.

I'm betting these lists look a little unbalanced huh. Fess up—alcohol's one of the easy buttons. Let's peel those layers back and quit being afraid of facing our fears. You know how to chase them away: acknowledge the truth, handle the emotions, apologize, accept it, move on, that's how to get naked, the real kind! No regrets—keep your clothes on, take your veils and masks off. It's time to get naked.

STAYING AWAKE

I have a convenient napping problem. I like to take naps starting at 8 pm. I'm not sure why, but for the longest time I would get home from work, get dinner done, clean up a bit and finally settle down around 7:30 for the evening. Now this should be the time for you to spend with your spouse and child, talking about the day, catching up on things. I would sit on the couch, lean over a bit and within thirty minutes, I'm snoring. Actually I don't snore, I sniggle. It's a cross between a giggle and a snore. It sounds much cuter.

I'm tired, I'm bored and I don't want to have any serious discussions. Once I woke up, usually around 10 pm, which was too late! So any naked conversations would be postponed. We would eventually get to them the 10th of never ever! I did not want to deal with serious topics.

Sleeping was my way of escaping. If I had been engaged enough and naked enough, I would have stayed awake and aware! I was neither.

- What are you using to escape? What is your "calgon, take me away?"

- Describe the last time you had too many drinks? What did that feel like?

- When do you have serious conversations with others? What do you do to prepare? Are you aware of the drain that they take on you physically and mentally? Are you aware that they might be festering, but never go away?

CHAPTER 10

LESSON 7: NAKED INFORMATION DOES NOT GET SHARED

Confess, you may be very scared of getting naked because you think there is something you've done or said or something that you "are" that is so terrible that if you reveal it you'll lose everything that you hold dear. What is the dearest thing that we hold? Just admit it, if we're naked about it, we're afraid that we'll lose "face." Our ego will be nicked and that would be brain freeze we don't want to deal with. So this fear you feel is attached to feelings of being "exposed." We spend tons of energy trying to cover up and to protect ourselves, which you now realize is the opposite of naked.

Naked spends little time at all "trying" to be anything. You just "are." You've seen several tips for naked, you know to ease in to it, you know to do it in a safe place and a very important rule to know and to keep is "naked information is not to be shared." Information should flow through you, not to you.

Information is just energy. You know what flows in us and sticks, all hot and juicy?? Gossip! Gossip has no place in wisdom because it doesn't contribute anything to our dreams. So what is it? It's just nothing, so don't waste your time or mind space collecting any of it.

Good rule of thumb, if information is used to gain power, influence or knowledge, its gossip! When someone gets naked with you, your goal and role is to just listen. You know it's their stage, their music, their dance. You don't help them by prodding, trying to get them to change any of the above, especially the pace at which they are comfortable revealing themselves. You just can't make other people get naked. Building naked relationships is about giving and receiving. It's about holding an open space for others to get naked. Being naked together absolutely builds synergy and energy. It's authentic and effortless and can lead you to places you've only dreamed existed.

Warning: there are definitely things not to do when someone's getting naked. You do not throw ice cold water on them. You do not try to help them get naked—they have to go at their own pace. It's their dance, so don't rush the show, please. You do not laugh at them because there is nothing worse than someone laughing at your naked parts! Just listen, maybe nod, just be a conduit for them.

Can you remember a time when someone might have been trying to get naked and you shut them down? If it's at the wrong time or place, it can be very uncomfortable and awkward. Perhaps you might owe them an acknowledgement or apology. Perhaps you might be able to rebuild that bridge. I'm guessing it's pretty broken.

GRATUITOUS NUDITY

You need to be on the lookout for "gratuitous nudity." Gratuitous, commonly defined as "not called for by the circumstances." This is an "oversharer." That person who is just hoping you will gossip with them, that you will ask all kinds of things they can't wait to share. You probably haven't even asked them anything. I really don't need to know about your neighbor being a cross-dresser, I don't need to know about all the drama in your mother's life or best yet, how difficult it is to keep your four cars clean. There is NO naked point to it. This is my definition of "Naked and no place to go!"

NAKED CONVERSATIONS

So how do you know if someone is going to be naked or FOS (figure this acronym out, ok). A couple of quick questions and answers will do the trick, and give you big clues:

Cocktail party conversation questions—

1. So how long have you lived here?
2. What's your favorite thing to do in town?
3. What's your favorite hobby?
4. What's your favorite type of music to listen to?

Remember you are looking to build relationships with other naked people. It's supposed to be a conversation. You will make deeper, more authentic connections and eventually your previous relationships that were not feeding your fabulous naked self will just fade away in to the sunset. Notice, these are not yes or no questions! Those are way too easy to have while being numb and dumb. It's very challenging to find yourself in a dead end conversation with a person that is not naked. How to get through it? Just stay naked. Be honest and sincere in your questions. Genuine interest is always appropriate and we have a radar for when it is not. You might want to think about your own interests and create your own "Hot Button" questions. It's really "fishing" for a connection, a connection to build momentum in the naked movement. Groups of people committed to letting those walls down and being honest in thoughts, actions and words. It starts with talking to each other. Open you heart, your mind and your mouth, preferably in that order.

CONSISTENT NAKEDNESS

Consistency counts. Naked should be the same no matter where you are or who you are with. It does not change according to your company, your weather or your mood. Now that you are becoming a naked expert, have you spent much time with someone that is not naked lately? You know who this person is because their opinion changes like their underwear. How annoying is that? Do you truly trust them at all? Ever find yourself thinking about what you are going to say when you're getting ready for a dinner party or a work event? How much energy do you spend trying to "fit in" or "blend in" or better yet "be in"? Naked just "is." No contemplation needed. You just know your own truths and you have the passion and compassion to know how and when to speak them. Remember your naked questions? Remember you're a magnet, use your questions to find those other naked people out there. Quit trying to say what you think they want you to say, dress like you think they want you to dress, and get naked.

∞ What does it feel like when someone shares something very personal and perhaps controversial with you? Are you tempted to share it with someone else? Are you tempted to be judgmental?

∞ Describe a time that you were getting naked with something and they responded in an inappropriate way. What did they do and how did you feel? Perhaps it was a parent that was less than supportive or a friend who was certain they knew what your opinion on a topic was going to be.

∞ Have you ever hurt someone deeply because you shared information that you should not have? How did you handle the situation and the changes to the relationship?

LESSON 8:
EVERYBODY WANTS TO GET NAKED;
THEY'RE JUST LOOKING FOR A SAFE PLACE TO DO IT

I am convinced. I talk to people everywhere I go (lots of strangers)! I believe that 90% of people truly do want to get naked. For the other 10%, the numb and dumber life is just too easy for them to want to change.

We were born naked, we played naked, we had wisdom, we discovered knowledge, and knowledge got too big for his britches and stomped on wisdom about the time we start making life changing decisions such as marriage, careers, family and friends. We get caught in the cotton candy vortex, get a few freeze warnings, drop into full hypothermia

(I'm melting, I'm melting) and realize that somewhere along this path we lost our naked self. The self that laughed, played, and was content. We look at where we are and what got us to the shut down, closed up cocoon we're in and we realize it was fears and unrecognized or unresolved feelings, and then what? What do we do? Well, most of us start searching for that secret potion or answer, in a club, in a church or some of us look in a book.

CLUBS AND ORGANIZED RELIGION

People are looking to avoid pain and they are looking for a safe place to be themselves. Be aware, these organizations offer both.

Have you ever been a member of one of them? What did you like about being a "member?" How long did you stay in? When and why did you leave? Was leaving your choice? We have already established that we are here to connect to others. This authentic connection and need to be "known" drives organizations. Call them clubs, gangs, tribes, whatever you call them; they are a group of people that come together with a common set of interests and beliefs. Throw in a hobby and you have a club, throw in an enemy and you have a gang and throw in set of rules or code of conduct and you have organized religion.

Clubs are everywhere. They start at a very young age. Remember creating special "clubs" when you were in elementary school? Maybe they were the K clubs, for girls whose names started with K's. We would make up any kind of club and it was normally so that we could have a group of people that were "in" and therefore if you weren't "in," you were "out."

This continues throughout our entire lives—in high school, fraternities or sororities, then country clubs, then private schools. It seems you can create a club around virtually any hobby, lifestyle choice or activity. I am ok with clubs as long as they are for community, relationship and are open to all. Clubs that come together with a passion and positive purpose can create a safe place for people to be authentic and get naked. One must be careful when their club decides they have a common enemy, at that point, all the energy can be spent focusing on the enemy and defeating the enemy in some way. This common enemy can create the "gang" mentality.

I have to talk about organized religion. It's tough to do it, but being that I have taken the naked oath, I have to discuss it. Churches can be incredible support structures and places for folks to get together. They were created for community and fellowship and a way to support members. Churches also can be full of rules and rituals. Rules and rituals commonly lead to relativity. We do this, we are good, you don't do this, you are bad. This is a flaw in the system. What starts as an act of love can quickly become a prison cell.

Your individual soul knows what it needs. Our spiritual relationships are individual. Any organization that does not allow that individual relationship or individual choices goes against the teachings directly. You should be free to think and speak freely within an organization when it is done with love. What if our purpose and self needs to grow and be fed and watered someplace else other than the local Baptist church? You will have a naked obstacle in your way.

Really think about this for a minute. If you have ever been in a PTA meeting where they were talking about another school's PTA fund raising program and how we "have to do better than them" stop and think, "am I in a gang?" Now, do you want to be a gang member?

Each of these organizations offers a place to fit in. When we fit in, we feel safe. When we feel safe, we let our guards down and we can breathe and rest and listen. We don't feel safe very often, but we want to. I know everyone wants to because they are desperately searching for a place to fit in. A place where they don't have to worry about being ridiculed, shamed or embarrassed. You can create a safe place. You can choose to accept people unconditionally. You can choose to forgive and forget. You can choose to give people a place where they will never be bullied or judged. You have that power. All you have to do is be yourself and allow others to do the same thing.

GETTING NAKED CAN HURT

I got a message today on facebook that read: "sometimes being naked hurts." Uh, yeah, sometimes it does.

Ever wax anything on your body? If you're not one of the privileged who has, have you ever ripped a band-aid off? Do you rip it quickly or do you do it little by little, hair by hair, yelping all the way? I'm not saying either is right or wrong, I'm just saying that both are painful. Some people would rather live with a frost warning for ten years as opposed to dealing with one quick brain freeze. I was very comfortable living in a slightly cold environment all the time, my former spouse was definitely a ripper off-er. I prefer to avoid the poodle with a very bad haircut thing. Poor poodles, they look so bare and unnatural with their hair shaved off, it just looks so incredibly overexposed.

I realize now that I never let the process of exposure, healing, and re-growth happen. If you can hold on through the pain-filled process called conflict, you will experience the healing that can happen when you expose yourself and let the love and light in. It's this experience that helps us build the courage to allow pain to be processed again, over and over. This is called resiliency.

I admit it, I was basically a streaker. Here you go "flash, flash" and then I covered back up so fast I couldn't feel any of the love around me, only the hurt of the confrontation. It's like shaving your legs and it growing back in fifteen seconds, it has no purpose, eventually you just quit doing it.

Here I am, an overexposed poodle, wounded and wobbling and along comes some positive feedback at work. Oh, this feels good, so much better than that yucky "truthful relationship" feeling. Ah, the balmy sunshine of career accolades, you've seen this roadmap before, and then it happens again. You fall right into the cotton candy vortex. You quickly find yourself once again at the wishing well, wishing you were someplace else all the time. The process of getting naked will involve pain. Pain is a catalyst for change. If we didn't already know this, we wouldn't have avoided all the pain that put us where we are today. Expect it, but know its purpose. Pain is a process, not a place you get stuck.

We are all looking for a safe place to get naked. We wander around like the bird in Dr. Seuss's *Are you my mother?*, and we look for missing pieces and parts of ourselves. When we've exhausted our resources and have no other easy fixes, we sit down and cry all the layers off, and we finally get still enough to hear wisdom and we start to slowly ease in to getting naked with ourselves. This is the first safe place we find. It is the nest we've been looking for and like little birdie sees, it's been there the whole time. We were just looking for something a little more spectacular, a little more glamorous, with some bling bling, but mostly we got blah, blah.

As we peel the layers off, we feel warmth and an energy familiar, yet so long ago forgotten. We start to get our real "stuff" back. We get laughter, we get smiles, we get relaxation, and we get contentment. We get our x-ray vision back and find empathy, sympathy and compassion. We get the eternal inoculation. You now know you can't catch someone else's pain, their struggle or their heartache by listening to them. You actually can be a pipe, where feelings run through you, not a pot where they stick to you. You will find yourself breathing deeper, smiling broader, and being more thankful for just being alive. You finally realize by making the choice to get naked, you made the choice to be born again. You made the choice to live life as it was meant to be lived—fully alive and present, grateful, content and free. You are naked.

 ℕ Describe the most unsafe place you have ever been. Who is there, what do they look like, how are they acting?

 ℕ What do you think to yourself when a stranger attempts to have a conversation with you?

 ℕ Do you talk to people on airplanes or are you the person who immediately opens a book and puts your nose in it?

CHAPTER 12

LESSON 9: NEVER PASS UP THE OPPORTUNITY TO GET NAKED—IT MAY NEVER PASS YOUR WAY AGAIN

S o we've experienced those moments when we have a sudden urge to get naked with someone, to be honest with someone, tell them how we feel (good or bad). In that moment, time stands still. It's the "I love you" moment or the "no, I really don't want to see you anymore" moment. These moments are slow motion at its slowest. When you look back you realize that you had the perfect chance to say... but you didn't because you were afraid, afraid of their reaction, afraid of the possible retaliation or the consequences. Do you usually take the easy way out and tell people what you think they want to hear? You realize this leads to an absolutely doomed "un-naked" relationship, right? Do you have the courage to get naked, acknowledge how you really feel and why? Maybe apologize that you know they are uncomfortable, and then accept where you are and move forward with an authentic relationship—no matter what the structure looks like?

Avoiding these real conversations usually happens when we are weary. We just don't know if we have the resiliency to have that honest conversation. I know I didn't when I had been napping for two hours. These opportunities happen in their own time and space for a reason. This is why we need to take care of ourselves (all the time) so we have the energy to make these opportunities life builders, not just another event you will have to right later on.

My mom recently had a total knee replacement surgery. She made the decision to go to a rehab facility for recovery and physical therapy for two weeks post-surgery. My mom is single and I am her primary support. She knows that I am incredibly busy and she tries very hard not to be a burden on me. She has this habit that I used to really want to kill her for. You see, she loves me true. She really really hates to be a burden on me in any way at all. Yet, she is human and she really does want to be loved and appreciated, like all humans do. So she never would tell me that she needed something. She would just wait and wait and wait and then it was an emergency situation. You see, no one would tell her "no" if it was an emergency situation. Hmm, kinda clever, actually.

My mother's life has been naked. As you know, she is a hopeless romantic that has followed true love over a cliff, climbed back up after heartache and disaster and she just keeps on going. She is never judgmental and really is a mother—when I ask her a question, she is kind enough to ask me "do you really want to know what I think?" Sometimes I don't, and that's ok too, she never tells me if that's the case, and she is never judgmental—ever. It used to be very inconvenient—this "emergency" path mom seemed to be on. Like the day we were in the emergency room after a horrendous accident that she had at my house which resulted in 90 stitches to her beautiful face, a broken wrist and several people asking if she had gone through a windshield. She was in a wheelchair being rolled back for yet another facial CT scan, and she was looking through her purse to get her credit card number out so I can pay her bill for her so its not late. Now, there are tons of people out there who are very healthy who wouldn't stop anything they were doing to pay a bill on time—but not my mom. It is more important to her to pay a bill on time than to have groceries in her house, to have gas in her car, or to have toilet paper. Oh, that's another story that I won't tell right now.

Mom was having knee replacement and asked me to go to the orientation with her to see the facility, learn how everything works, etc. Now, my mom is young. She didn't physically or mentally need me to be with her to learn these things, so it must really be that "other" thing she needed, support. I had an internal battle "Uggh, but I'm really busy," "you must SHOW people that you love them." Ok, I'm naked, I'm going with her pseudo cheerfully. Hey, just because you commit to naked doesn't mean it's always an easy decision. She is the youngest person there by a good fifteen years and I am the youngest by twenty-five. The immediate impression of the center really threw me for a loop. There were many elderly people there who were not in good health. They were getting rehab services, living in extended care rooms; they were beyond middle age and zoomed right into the golden ages. I was very aware of the entire surrounding and what it meant, from the smells, to the sights and sounds, to the reality of my mothers' health, to my own parental role, to my own mortality. These thoughts all hit me hard.

If I was not naked, here's what would have hit me, "I can't believe I'm here. This is inconvenient. Why didn't she come by herself?" I would have been generally in a terrible mood and blamed it on my mom and resented her for "inconveniencing" me. Notice how I was taking no responsibility for being there on my own. This is what happens when we do things we don't want to do—we just get resentful and snippy and blame other people. So I took a deep breath and had and AHAA moment. I realized that what I actually felt was very guilty for being healthy and not appreciative enough. Normally I would have shut down to it all, thought about how quickly I could get out of there, and hope that I didn't catch any of their emotions through my armor.

I made the choice to be here with her because I love her. I do love her, no matter how it may manifest itself, and that is why I was there, it was not about me. I realized how uncomfortable I was first. It was that antsy familiar feeling of uncomfortable that I have learned to recognize. I then went inside myself, breathed, stayed present and thought about how they must all feel, so scared, so uncertain. Remember, I am pretty new to this "how do I really feel" game, so I definitely had to stop and purposefully take steps to become self-aware. I suspect some people are good at this and do not have to be so intentional with their actions. You and I will get there, once we practice being naked long enough. Naked does move from something that you do to something that you become. I am grateful for that promise.

At this moment in the rehab facility, I wondered how my inner sunshine might help them if I let it shine a little. I wondered if I might be able to ease a little discomfort of theirs just by being myself and I started talking to every one I could. I was not going to avoid eye contact, I was not going to avoid those that looked busy. I went right up to them and introduced myself, a lost art, by the way. I asked when they would be having surgery. I told them I hoped it went well, and I meant it. I pretended I was Dolly Parton, truly, and it was much easier as her than me, but to them, I might as well have been her. This was all I could possibly do for them.

The ultimate gift is the gift of our true selves. Naked people realize it and recognize it and celebrate it. I lost fear of losing my precious positive attitude (because it is precious) and the energy changed, it grew to meet my needs and the needs of the room, like magic!

We went for a building tour with a small group of people planning their post-surgery stays. When we stepped on to the elevator there was a lovely little lady with a walker who had a twinkle in her eye. I openly made eye contact with her and smiled. She then told me she "loved my shoes." She was incredibly perky, and at least ninety years old. Now, I think I failed to mention that Ms. Sensitivity was wearing 4" platform giraffe-print pony hair shoes. So now you have a better picture of the guilt and embarrassment of sitting in a room filled with hip and knee replacement patients. I got naked with this lady instantly.

I smiled and said, "I have to admit I feel a little bad wearing them around here." She said, "oh, honey, you just better be careful, a snake might climb up your leg and try to mate with them." Honest to God, that is what she said to me. Well, I burst out laughing. Everyone in the elevator did. I laughed so hard and true, and that is a moment I will never forget. I honestly felt such genuine love from this lady with no expectations in return. It is just a feeling that once you know what it is, you seek it out everywhere and you want to give it. It is a gift. You truly don't ever know where joy will find you or how. I encourage you to quit trying to figure everything out and plan every minute of your life! Have no expectations, just wonder what might happen today and smile at people. Not that fake, "have a nice day" smile, but that real "life is grand" smile that makes people think you know something they don't—because you do. You're starting to know the secret of freedom and hopefully they will ask you about it and you can tell them to "get naked." It just feels better.

NAKED IN ASIA

I recently spent fourteen days in Asia with my graduate class. This was my first naked trip. I've had many "un-naked" trips. You know, the ones where you plan out every second and every outfit and every perfect conversation! This trip was naked in several ways:

- I was not in charge or control.
- I had never been to these three countries in Asia before.
- I didn't speak the language.
- My title, industry and income meant nothing.
- I went as a peer, with no seniority at all.
- I don't look like anybody else there.

Basically, I'm a girl with a blonde ponytail. Well, that girl sees everything differently than Ms. Control Freak or Ms. Business Executive. She just gets to "be" on an adventure. There is complete freedom from expectations, if she can handle it. She has no past to consider, no need to think about the future, someone else has planned it. Have you ever been in this position? Ever? It is a very eerie place to be. It's like being in a vastness of open possibility and no road map and no obstacles. It's like being on a train with no track. I imagine it's like some former prison inmates who have a very difficult time readjusting to being free. They are just not used to having options and choices without strings attached. It's at first a very ungrounded place to be, like you're suspended in between something and can go in any direction. It was scary, I realized how uncomfortable I was, which is the first indicator that there's a naked opportunity!

This trip was with real people, twenty-one graduate students, all different and incredibly unique in their own ways. On this trip, we were children again with x-ray vision. We were kind and generous and patient and we laughed and talked and we genuinely loved each other as we were. I started to see people not as good or bad, but just as different and adjusted my exposure accordingly. We had no distractions of would be's or should be's. It was just us.

We bonded on common respect and compassion and we saw the world as much bigger than ourselves. When we came back to the states, we were all more naked than when we left. Titles didn't mean as much, salaries didn't mean as much, the conversations, the memories, all those things that could not be taken away, they meant everything. We didn't buy things for each other, we didn't spend money on clothes or lavish meals, but we have invaluable memories of the laughs while watching someone eat strange food, including a breakfast of Budweiser and Doritos! When was the last time you lived with anyone other than your immediate family for fourteen days, eating every meal together, seeing each other every single day? Hold on to the memories, the sounds, the pictures, the colors and the smells. They cannot be taken away.

Naked sees who you are and seeks to connect with no expectations or needs. We realized that this is possible and whether we realized it at the time or not, we found hope. We found hope that this could be done anywhere, at anytime, if people wanted to. Regardless of title, gender, country or religious views. We saw the local people living their daily lives. Parents were walking children to school, mothers were grocery shopping, teenagers were hanging around at the mall texting each other. These people want the best for their lives and their children's lives, just like we do. We all may eat different types of food, wear different clothes, drive different cars, but we are all connected. In more ways than not, we are all the same. We could have a naked world, if enough people wanted to.

Naked Notes

- Tell me a little about an opportunity to tell the truth that you passed up, what were the consequences?

- How often do you conveniently let people believe things that you know are not accurate?

- Regret. What does this word mean to you?

CHAPTER 13

LESSON 10:
GETTING NAKED
IS THE EASY PART

So you have no idea how bad I wish I could say, "Whoo Hoo! You did it! You're naked! You hit the bulls eye, finished the race, you get a gold medal!" But I can't, because you're going to find out, getting naked is the easy part.

2010 was a whirlwind year for me. I'll always refer to it as my whoo hoo year. (Thanks Cindy!) It was a year-long journey of ragged edges, swollen eyelids, hours of prayer, and not the pretty poetic kind, either—the bitchy, moaning, yelling, cursing, crying out loud kind. I visited four foreign countries, lost that last 10 pounds, wrote a book (which I've also learned is the easy part), made some real friends, did an internet radio show, started a blog, website and facebook fan page, and pitched my concept to all types of media, in person! I was in a constant ebb and flow of ripping off a band-aid and then moving forward by getting naked and ripping off another band-aid. It was a constant cycle of pushing myself to the edge of total terror and fear and then holding on for dear life. Throughout all of this, a funny thing happened—I grew each and every time and I got to know my naked self.

My year ended with the whoo hoo of a whirlwind trip to India, which was incredible, but then I came home and everything screeched to a halt. It was a very freaky thing, like a switch just flipped the carnival ride off, while I was at the top of the Ferris wheel. At the time, I had no idea why this happened. I blamed it on the holidays, the hustle and bustle, the graduation ceremony. I had several things that were coming to a conclusion. In naked retrospect, perhaps I have a few ideas why everything just stopped.

I realized that as all of these events were taking place I subconsciously began creating my own expectations of being "that" girl. At this point, we both know the drama attached to expectations!

"That" girl that finally finds herself and instantly her incredibleness is recognized and heralded by the entire universe.

"That" girl that is the next JK Rowling and is suddenly on Oprah-

"That" girl that meets her true soulmate when she spills a coke on him dashing through one of many airports.

"That" girl who is finally rewarded for all of her good deeds—time for the karma jackpot!

I put all of this in motion, I got naked, I told the truth, I got uncomfortable. So bring it on, all of it, show me why all of this has happened to me this year!

I waited… and I waited… and cars broke down and parents got sick and I gained those last 10 pounds back and I spent new Year's Eve "unmated" with a girlfriend wearing my silver ankle bracelet covered in tiny silver bells that I bought in India as a good luck charm. Hey, at least I was not lying on the coach again this year! I was trying desperately not to think about those 10 pounds and the days just ticked on in my same job. My son acted like a teenager and I acted like an irate mother and I wasn't actually sure I could finish the book. I was not even looking at the book anymore. I had flatlined—I wasn't leaving the house much. I wasn't depressed, just hibernating, until I got those 10 pounds back off. My counselor said this is what a person's real life looks like, routine, sometimes there's no woo hoo. I will never ever forget my spontaneous answer: "Not my life. This is not my life!" and it was a huge smack in the face because I suddenly realized I had been there before.

For all the miracles I had seen, the tears I had cried, the love I had felt, here I was again, throwing the same "boat tantrum," saying, "where's my prize?"

Suddenly, I just knew that this was real life, every second, every minute and every hour. I licked my wounds, stuffed my giant ego in my car and drove home to throw myself down on the yoga mat and say those always very scary and always very revealing words, "What am I afraid of right here, right now?"

Like you, I humbly got naked again with myself, one AHAA moment at a time. I acknowledged fear of failure and fear of success. I acknowledged the people in my life that were hurting me and the ones who were helping me. I told myself the truth and then I handled the emotions, all of them: shame, guilt, and anxiety. I apologized to myself for whoo-hooing myself ragged and trying to once again "get there." I quit looking around airports for "him" and I quit wishing I was on a date with him when I was curled up on a chair on a Friday night at home and I accepted where I was today, this minute, on this shore.

You know, maybe one day I'll be "that" girl, and maybe I won't. But for today, at this moment, I'm finally in love with "this" girl, naked, and that's how being honest really can change your life forever.

⌑ Who are you?

⌑ Who do you want to be?

⌑ Can you be honest, starting with yourself first?

⌑ Are you ready to have naked relationships, starting with yourself first?

⌑ Do you want to know what freedom feels like?

CHAPTER 14

LIVING A NAKED LIFE: NAKED THOUGHTS AND STORIES

I've learned so many things over the last year while I was learning to be honest and getting naked. I want to share them with you, as random naked thoughts and stories. From seeing things as we want to see them, all the way to how in the world did we choose our careers, hopefully you will find comfort and wisdom in knowing that you are never alone when you are naked. Find a safe place so that you can be a safe place. Be true. Be you. Be naked.

NAKED EYES JUST SEE THINGS DIFFERENTLY

I had the pleasure of listening to Craig Wynette, chief creative officer at Proctor and Gamble speak at my graduate program. What an awesome job, creative officer. You have visions of this creative Einstein type that just exudes a combination of Bill Gates and DaVinci.. He walked into the room, a little disheveled and drinking a Mountain Dew. He was a pretty normal guy. His message was basically that unlike what most people think, we do not have a thinking problem, we have a seeing problem. We see what we think, not what is actually there.

There is a lot of evidence to support this theory, with multiple people studying the left and right sides of the brain and how we use them. Daniel Pink's *A Whole New Mind* talks very factually about how right-brainers are going to rule the world. I believe that wisdom resides in that right side of the brain. You see what you "think" you see because we are human and our know it all operates very efficiently at lightening speeds and if you think "flowerpot" you will actually start drawing what your mind thinks a flowerpot looks like, not what the flowerpot actually looks like. Get the picture? It first categorizes what you "know" before it lets you learn something new for the database. I think this is why I have such a hard time with foreign languages, I just can't attach it to something I already know and that much new information just rocks my little world.

We also see things the way we want to see them in order to justify our reactions. As you get naked, you remove the layers you used to see things through. "Rose colored" glasses really do exist, but we have about twenty-five pairs that we filter everything through. When you get naked you separate facts from fiction—it's like an egg separator, separating the white from the yolk. You look at things not without assumptions (because we're human) but with acknowledgement of our own bias, this is being self aware, and then allowing yourself to go deeper. Slow down, ask yourself some naked questions, like "is this really true?" How do I know it's true? Take things down to the basic facts only. Let it settle before you choose your response. Detach yourself and ask what am I feeling? Is it real? Is it sadness, is it anger, is it loneliness or fear? We are woefully unaware of more than two emotions, happy and sad, basically good or bad. We do not innately have the ability to recognize feelings in a detached way. Everything is so incredibly personal when you are the center of the universe, isn't it? By getting naked, you are in the process of realizing that you actually aren't the sun and everything doesn't revolve around you and your personal comfort and pleasure.

NAKED KNOWS THE 3 F WORDS: FEELINGS, FEARS AND FACTS

When you are in the throes of getting defrosted and the challenges are great and the pain tough, please remember it is normal. The process is normal and predictable.

When you are naked, there is nothing that anyone can take away from you. Have you realized that you are afraid of losing "stuff"? Its one of the reasons you're not naked now right now. It reminds us we're really not in charge or in control. This is a very uncomfortable feeling for most people and the life they build trying to avoid the discomfort is amazing. There are many reasons that we close down. Fear is a big part of our conscious and unconscious actions and reactions. Feelings, hmm, they are really scary. This may be shocking, but we have more than two feelings (happy and sad) and all feelings aren't sub-feelings to these two.

THE FIRST F WORD: FEELINGS

Now really think about this for a minute, can you distinguish the difference between sad and lonely? How? Can you distinguish the difference between happy and content? How about happy and giddy or silly or excited? How about stressed, anxious and excited? They are all energy and there are very subtle differences in how we feel them, express them and project them out in to the world. This week pick one day and stop every hour or so and reflect on how you are actually feeling. Look deep. Breathe, shut your eyes and see how many feelings you can identify. Are you anxious, nervous, peaceful, worried? What does each one feel like? Remember a feeling is something that you **feel** in the body, not **think** in your head. Really notice the difference. When you have one day's worth, make a commitment to being more aware of these. Notice your reaction to the feelings—what can you learn about yourself with this information?

Feelings can be very uncomfortable, especially during the early thawing out period of naked. They are down right scary. One opposite of naked is controlled. We all try to control ourselves all the time so that our feelings do not overwhelm us, but then we hit that death spiral and feel very horrible, quickly. It can feel like falling into a bottomless pit of darkness. Remember when you first learned to swim? You were so afraid you were going to sink right to the bottom of the water. What did they teach you to do first? FLOAT. Don't struggle and you won't sink. Don't panic and you can float forever. The same is true with our feelings. When you struggle and try extremely hard to stuff them down and not acknowledge them, it is a bottomless pit. You can't push them down far enough. This is one reason we have a tough time with compassion. Come one, we're human. We're struggling with our own junk, why would we want to feel someone else's?

We are terribly afraid we're going to feel someone else's feelings, their pain and their suffering, but we actually don't. We're a bridge, a conduit of sorts. We actually feel compassion for that person, an ability to connect because we are both human, the feelings run through us, they don't stay in us when they are not happening to us. It's a phenomenon really. It's a trick, smoke and mirrors. We can't catch someone's feeling, they can influence our feelings, but that's a choice. Remember this: you can remain in a place where you feel compassion, which is connected, without "catching" actually feelings.

You have two parts to this equation, first is the feeling itself, second is the reaction to the feeling, which is where most of us get confused. We think the reaction is the feeling, if I am sad and then I get angry with another person because they ask me to do something, I may tell myself I am angry, but anger is actually the reaction that I am having to being sad. Think about grief at a funeral home. There is no way that you can possibly feel what the person that loses someone feels, but when you have compassion, you have a general love and appreciation for the human condition, which grieves losses. See the difference? By staying in that space for the person, you allow their grief to flow through them and their individual process of grieving can continue to take place. You can connect to their feeling of grief without having a reaction to it. With practice, you can do the same thing with your feelings. Feeling is not optional when you are naked, but our response is always a choice. Compassion is reaching out to others to help their feelings flow, not get stuck! Don't forget to start with compassion for yourself! Through this connection process, we can fully realize we are all human. Shocking.

FEAR: THE SECOND F WORD

Our two greatest fears are the fear of failure and the fear of success. One for what it does to us and one for what it does to others around us. How can two opposite things hold us so captive? How can this keep the light of truth so hidden? You see, the big secret is that the light, which is exposure, is what melts the fear. It's what dissolves and contains knowledge where it was meant to be. Knowledge wasn't meant to hurt us, you see we have that pesky "free will." Ironically, we use knowledge to keep us from being free, this is a self imposed prison sentence. It's hard to trust wisdom when for years you have literally been brainwashed into believing that your value is compared to some picture of what a "successful" person is supposed to look like.

Let's be honest, it's hard for a twelve year old to hear that voice within. The voice that is saying, "be kind, turn the other cheek," when you feel lonely, isolated and are being picked on at school everyday. It is tough to stay full of light when the world can be so dark. Thank God there are kind teachers who encourage and love the children, who listen to the voice. I was one of these outsiders. I have had several teachers who have played very influential roles in my life because they believed in me enough to pay attention to me. They helped me with homework when I had no help and they gave me lunch money without me having to ask.

The challenges are enormous to being naked as a mature adult, I'm not even sure you can stay completely naked through the teenage stages because of all the constant change. Change is a great creator of fear.

At any given time, we have an equal chance of change producing a better result and a worse result. Why do we always prepare for the worst? Again, knowledge is trying to protect us from pain based on past experiences. If you have ever experienced pain because something changed, you will struggle against change the rest of your life if you do not become "aware" of this pattern and get naked.

THE THIRD F WORD: FACTS

Call them cold hard, call them incontrovertible truth, call them crap, it doesn't matter what you call them, they just are. We don't usually want to deal with the facts. There is no drama or emotion tied to them. Facts don't have a story attached to them. They just are. When I am rocking and rolling on the roller coaster of fears and feelings, I have to stop myself and ask the question, "What are the facts?" They are usually short, simple and not what I want to hear. I have so entangled the actual facts with my own stories and interpretations and assumptions that it truly is like weeding a garden. You know somewhere underneath all the weeds, the underbrush, the thorns, the trash, there is something that is alive and true.

We have been trained since we were very young to anticipate, be proactive and to please. This causes us to want to jump to conclusions so we can solve a problem, avoid an issue, and keep moving moving moving. We rarely hear what someone is saying to us because we are too busy formulating our answer to their question in our minds. We are already planning our reactions, and we get disappointed if they don't actually go where we expect them to with the conversation, because we have a great answer or response ready for them! Our response, of course, will prove us to be worthy, smart and witty to them, but mostly to ourselves. Even if we don't finish their sentences for them out loud, we are doing it in our head. We cannot hear the facts for the fear that we will have an unworthy answer. This fear pushes us to simultaneously play out the conversation in our heads.

Great leaders routinely struggle with listening and with decoding facts. Leaders must make quick decisions with limited information and rely on their own intuition and abilities to make a gut call. This pressure and short timeline creates a great sense of urgency to complete a task and move the never-ending list of "nexts." Leaders are often paid big bucks to fill in the blanks around the facts, to be future tellers. Facts do not lie to us or tell us what we want to hear. We can use facts as a springboard to self-awareness or a diving board to the vortex of fears and feelings, deep into the river of drama and pity.

Time and patience are needed to weed through all the drama and the fears to see the facts. I have found that when I step back and look at the facts and become an observer, detached from the situation, I can see the facts much more quickly. If I let myself get pulled into the feelings involved it's quicksand, and it drags you deeper and deeper.

For example: the facts may be that the office manager cried after having her month end reporting information questioned by the client. Did you jump to the automatic conclusion that the client made the office manager cry? This is a very common jump. As a leader, if I acted on this assumption I might call the client, I might say things about respecting our office manager and I might be very defensive. I would have been making assumptions and lashing out at the client because I felt bad for the office manager.

An alternative approach would be to deal with the facts. The first place to start is with asking open-ended questions. I can say to the office manager, "tell me a little bit about your conversation with the client," With effective questions I will be able to hear from the office manager the facts of the situation from her perspective. I might find out that the office manager cried because she felt bad about a mistake she made in the reports and hated to disappoint the client. I might find out that she cried because the client told her that they were leaving the group and would no longer be working with her. The point is, you do not know the facts until you have the courage to take the time and effort to inquire and find out what the facts are. You must ask.

The next time you find yourself in a whirlwind drama of fears and feelings, stop and ask yourself, "what are the facts? what do I really know?" Stop the stories in your head, they are not necessarily true and they are wasting your time and energy.

THE WAFFLES

My decisions became so much easier when I became naked, making them just felt better. Now don't be confused, the execution of my decisions are just as complicated, but the actual decisions are pretty easy. Caution: do not confuse these two processes. In the past, I started many "plans" before I truly made the decision. I was trying to swim with one foot firmly planted on shore, just in case I changed my mind. As I paddled furiously with my arms, and fluttered with one leg, one leg anchored me firmly in just the spot where the waves broke and crashed on the store. I was committed enough to be in deep water and the waves continued to crash right on my head, over and over and over. I was stuck in the exact same spot, but the good news was (or so I thought) when I got tired enough, I could actually stand up and walk back to shore, I was definitely hedging my bets. I realize that most of these "pseudo-decisions" were made at the wrong time, at the swell of the wave, the point where the tension is the greatest. Every wave breaks, wait for the break to take action (the right action) and then swim like hell over the wave and to the smooth waters on the other side.

My most recent struggle with the waffles was my struggle to actually finish this book. I was stuck. The manuscript was completed and I was dragging my feet to get the editing done. People would ask me, "when is the book coming out?" "Still working on it," would be my answer, still working, still working. The truth was, I was still looking at the book, that's about it. I had a case of the waffles—am I doing this thing or not? Either swim, or get your butt back on to the shore, but quit riding this wave. I asked myself some naked questions: Are you waffling on the value of telling the truth?, Hell no! Are you waffling on the ease of making the decision to tell the truth?, Hell no! Are you waffling on the miracle of what you see in other people's lives? Hell no! Then what are you? The answer came, "afraid." Plain and simple, "I'm afraid." What if this entire process has just been a fleeting hobby, Kelly's most recent attempt at following a whim? And again, the answer came, "so what if it is?" What could happen if the book is completed? People could read it and like it or people could read it and hate it or people could not read it at all. The fact was I would never know what this book was meant to do if I was afraid to finish it, and I chose to have faith. Faith always conquers fear and I made a decision and I swam like hell to get over the wave. Each stroke got easier as I focused only on completing the book and gave no energy to any of the what if's or maybe's.

When you are naked your intention is to live a life honest in actions, thoughts and words. When you are faced with a decision, tell yourself the truth about what you really want. Period. That's it. There are real benefits of telling yourself the truth, of being naked:

- By telling yourself the truth you no longer waste energy on the "waffles," the vicious cycle of should have's and could have's.

- By telling yourself the truth you no longer waste energy investing in dead end relationships.

- By telling yourself the truth you empower yourself to make the decisions that you want to; thus creating momentum to achieve your goals 100% of the time.

If you have a compelling reason to make a different decision, that's ok as well, but take equal responsibility for that decision, then it is still your truth. A quick example of how this works:

- Think about what is real and what is part of the convenient story that you are telling yourself to sabotage your efforts to be free and uncommon. Separate the story and the facts.

- Deal only with the facts.

I'm not saying this is fun, pretty or easy. I cry many times when I think of the things that I love that can be taken away.

Fear says "You might lose a car, a job, a limb or a child."

Feelings say "Pain, torment, be prepared, be scared, shut down, don't get too close, covet, hold on serve and protect.

But the facts are: "Things happen in the present. It's where wisdom lives moment to moment. You will breathe. You will choose to. Your eyes will blink, your body will live. You choose the reaction that is attached to a feeling at all times. It's not easy, but really let this sink in. We do choose—I can feel sad and not fall into depression, this is a response I choose. I can feel pain and choose to be happy, this is a response I choose. I can feel disappointed and choose not to be angry, this is a response I choose.

Feelings are temporary, they can change quickly. They do have to be acknowledged so you can choose to allow them to flow through you. What I've found is that by "exposing" our feelings they lose their power over us. That little voice of knowledge (Mr. Know It All) eventually shuts up and learns his place in the universe. He is to be called on for a fact, by wisdom at the moment you need the information, I don't need all the other color commentary, that's good old fashioned drama. That's the way it is supposed to work.

Love, happiness and joy are not things that float on the wind and you just happen to be lucky and they drop on your head for the day. You create them, on demand, at anytime. All feelings are energy. You are the source, the maker and the generator. But we don't trust that we can do that on demand, that joy and happiness are always available to us. That's just too much responsibility. We would rather rely (or blame) someone else for our (lack of) happiness, (lack of) contentment and general place in life.

NAKED WARNING: SOMETIMES YOU JUST FIND YOURSELF NAKED

How energy is harnessed and used determines it value. Think of a lightening bolt vs. a 120 volt circuit running your computer. Energy is itself not "good" or "bad." We've talked about exposure in the painful way. So, when hypothermia hits full blast, with no warning and it blows right in like the North Pole, sometimes naked finds you. Maybe there weren't red flags of brain freeze, you've been on a very neat and well-defined pathway giving you accolades and pleasures and success and you really have no reason at all to explain why suddenly nothing is the same in your life. Unfortunately, this does happen. Suddenly, cleanly and savagely it can burn everything to the ground in a nanosecond.

As humans, we're very attached to things that are "true" because it gives us an external beacon that we can align too outside our own core values and beliefs. This external beacon, We weren't the ones to select it and to think of it so we're in many ways absolved of any personal responsibility if it later proves to be "untrue," but, once we claim something true, we demand that it stays that way. This is one reason that we have so many different church denominations. They were created when groups of people held strongly to their beliefs when others felt a different truth or need to change. If it doesn't stay true it is a reminder of many things we don't like. Everything changes, you're not in control, you're not the center of the universe, and you know all those things that keep old "know it all" in business. We spend excessive amounts of energy daily trying to "keep" things true, and avoid change at all costs. The beacon moves and we don't like it. Again, you see this in many organized religions that remove the real personal relationship from the equation. Think of how the world might change if we loosened up a little on what we "know."

Byron Katie has a great book, *Loving What Is.* This book addresses the question, "what if what you think is true, is not?" On her website, Katie says:

"I discovered that when I believed my thoughts, I suffered, but that when I didn't believe them, I didn't suffer, and that this is true for every human being. Freedom is as simple as that. I found that suffering is optional. I found a joy within me that has never disappeared, not for a single moment. That joy is in everyone, always."

This is a great way to practice separating facts from fiction and facts from feelings. Many great inventions and occurrences have happened because people have challenged what we thought was true. In order to do that we have to be very confident in our naked selves, otherwise we spend all of our energy being judgmental and comparing ourselves and our stuff to everyone one else, and there's no room for something new!

Sometimes that which is called true and annoys us is what we may be called to dive deeper into. How about the "that's just the way it is" that we hear all the time at work? How about the "sorry, we can't do anything about that" when you file a complaint with a store. Make a list of the things that annoy you. Things that make you go, "Hmmm." Check out Katie's website and see what insight you might gain from her four questions.

CAREER—WHAT WE WANT TO BE WHEN WE GROW UP

How about a job? When did we start obsessing with a career? Speaking of our fear of having something taken away—success really is a two-sided sword. I'm not sure where the word career even came from. According to Wikipedia it is: "an individuals' course or progress through life." Anything here about job, vocation, money? Those are things we have just attached to the word. When did the transition take place from having a vocation to having a career? Then add "purpose" to the mix, so let me get this straight. I used to just need a vocation to have money for the basics, food, shelter, clothing, etc. and my "career" was to be human, listen to my heart, be kind, love, be in relationships—then enter a few hurts, unresolved roadblocks and construction zones, and we shut down. We turn to the career as much more than a vocation.

We start feeling the love from the vocation in many ways: more money, positive attention, and you really start liking it. With this career thing you get a whole package good feelings, security, built in friendships to socialize with (because you're working all the time together), two kids and a dog…no, sorry, that's not this package. Every once in a while, when you get really still, you might hear that tiny faint whisper, the one that says, "hey, is this all there is to life?" Of course you ignore it and say, "pass me another all expenses paid trip to anywhere away from my current life!" When you are numb, you can't feel the pleas of wisdom at all.

For many of us, the "career" is the new "Calgon, take me away!" You're never home, you never rest, you're always doing something, blah, blah, blah, sound familiar? You say to yourself, "I have to do all this stuff, who else will do it?" "I don't have a choice." We simply compress all of these activities into a box and pretend that doing these "things" must be our purpose in life (which is obviously to just "do" something, anything, because we are so incredibly good at that!). Right—this is my purpose, right? To do all this stuff? I AM LIVING MY PURPOSE DAMNIT! Right? I do take care of myself, I schedule a massage once a month, after work and before baseball practice and not on the 3rd of 4th week of the month because of client meetings. But I am on the right path, right? Sound familiar?

Oops, except that exposure thing hits. Oops, a couple of roadblocks, like a new boss. A construction zone, like your spouse has had it with your work schedule, or your parent's health is failing. This is life for most of us. It's what we see, hear and feel. Where did we fall? When did fear take over and we go on auto-pilot? How did we get so far off course? I suspect it's not a moment, but a slow drifting. Drifting one decision at a time, the choices we make to ignore feelings because we just don't have time to deal with them.

Needier than a two year old

I remember how frustrating it was when my two year old was sick, or dirty, or wanted to play when I was tired or "busy." My two year old seemed so needy. What I have come to realize is that I was the needy one. I was much more needy than any two year old. I needed to know I was smart. I needed to know I would never worry about having money for food. I need to know I could have my hair highlighted, my tires replaced, and my annual beach vacation. I needed these things desperately to prove

I was worthy, worthy of a place on this earth, worthy of a place in the "business world." I needed to be one of those women I read about in the Harold Robbins novels growing up. You know the one, the come from nothing to world domination with street smarts, business savvy and a hot body. You know, the trash to class story. I was certainly on my way to stardom in a trashy novel for sure. I would complain to my mom, about being a momand she always said, "I know it seems really hard right now, but you're going to miss this." And she was right. I do miss my son being two, because I hardly remember it and that it sad.

I don't miss things now, I try to love big and open and recognize the signs of resentment creeping in when my workday is inconvenienced because my son is sick and I stay home with him. I see snow days as a blessing because there really won't be many more where he asks me to go out and sled with him or to build a snowman. Today he asked me to take him to the mall, and it was obviously not in a stroller, and I did, because I know, one day soon, I'm going to miss this.

Lots of times I have felt like my son might not love me (don't we all feel that way sometimes) but he has a way of leaving me this message everywhere. I'm the one who has the problem, I never slowed down to see it before. So when I look up from my desk at work at the white board covered with the 18 month strategic plans for the company and right in the middle my son has written "I love you mom" and made a heart out of the magnet stick pins, my heart fills to the brim with what is important—true love. So every time I see it, I celebrate. It is a gift, even if it is carved in the coffee table, or written on his bedroom furniture with a black Sharpie marker. I would rather recall a memory with a huge smile on my face than to miss an opportunity that I could have had, but gave away. When you are numb, you are giving away more than you realize and there really are no take backs.

GIVEAWAYS AND TAKE BACKS

What are you giving away? What are you not noticing because you are closed off and shut down? Whatever it is, I promise eventually you will look back and realize you missed it and there are some things where there are no take backs allowed.

Common things we ignore:

- Time conflicts with work assignments and personal wants, like a child's school program.

- Do you numb down and tell your children you have to go to work, you have no choice, you have to make money? And then quickly move on? Many people do this. We expect a child to have their emotional needs addressed with a factual explanation. This just doesn't work. When you choose not to address the emotional parts of an issue you're sending the message that those feelings are not important or shouldn't be addressed. Do you really want your children to be numb too? Tell them how you feel. That's how they learn to tell people how they feel. It's so simple, but not easy.

So try this: acknowledge the feelings first. "I know you're really excited about this program. Tell me about it," and then listen. "I'm really disappointed that I have to miss it. I love you and know you will do great." Then add facts, "I have to meet with a client that night," then add love, "but I look forward to you telling me all about it when we both get home."

When we ignore and numb down we teach our kids to do that as well. Be honest with your kids or they will become stuffers. This will manifest itself in generation after generation if we do not stop the cycle.

FEAR OF LOSING STUFF

So what can people really take away from you? Remember that the fear of losing "stuff" motivates action. Go back to your naked story you did at the very beginning of the book. Take a look at the list. How many of those things are actually objects? I drive a BMW, ok, the BMW is a thing. It can be taken away, yes. That's not a part of who you are it's something that you have. Remember that who you actually are cannot be taken away from you. What actions are you consistently doing to keep from "losing" that object? You may not have any, if not, congratulations you pass the attachment test.

We conveniently get attached to "things" that cause us to have to stay in places and do things that we "say" we don't want to. "I can't quit my job, we couldn't keep our cars (all 6 of them)," or "I can't leave this relationship, who would I talk to?" You mean yell at, talk bad about and generally be miserable with. Remember, the opposite of naked (freedom) is to be controlled (caged in) with no choices or options.

Do you really ever have no choice? Perhaps you have a choice but the preferred choice has too many negative consequences. All choices have consequences and you determine if the outcome is good or bad, which themselves are relative terms depending on the individual. How are you making your decisions? Are you looking at short-term pain, long-term gain? Are you looking at the comfort or discomfort levels of each choice? Are you looking at how the choices will impact others? Each of us makes decisions based on unconscious factors if we are not living a life with clearly defined intentions.

The truth is you always have a choice, keep digging and asking the questions to get down to the root issue and situation. Look at the truth, touch it, feel it, breathe it. From the foundation of truth you can make real decisions based on who you really are, not on attachment to "things" "titles" or mostly "lies", the ones you conveniently keep telling yourself.

I don't like to be told no, especially by me! "No, you can't have that glass of wine, no you can't eat that third piece of pizza." Don't know about you but all of this constriction makes me down right pissy. It makes me antsy and rebellious. I am uncomfortable because of a convenient lie I think to keep telling myself, several convenient lies actually. These lies are: I can eat what I want to and not gain weight, I can drink several glasses of wine and not be moody from the sugar, I can just snack on this and a little bit of that and maintain my weight. These are all convenient lies. Thankfully, when I got naked these were a few of the easy ones. I found a way to deal with these lies by telling myself the honest truth, I finally quit kidding myself, I always have a choice and sometimes I choose to eat more than I need and drink more than is healthy, so what? I made the choice and I move forward. I don't stuff or numb down the consequences of the action. I'm up a few pounds for a few days, I ride out the mood swing for a couple of days, it was my decision and they are my consequences. I learned this was a better way to ride out my feelings that the hundreds of dollars spent on post-binge weight loss plans and one very bad haircut! No more running on auto-pilot with those feelings in the cock pit.

When you continue to run on auto-pilot with no "home base" you end up "wherever" and then you complain about where you are and how you got there. We have knowledge to thank for this. Wisdom is just happy to be here today, in this moment, with clothes, food, shelter, not dead. It's knowledge that is the great animator, the storyteller. We very quickly get carried away with our own stories. The fact is: things happen and are going to happen (duh) and they may hurt (duh) and people might laugh at you and call you names (duh) and they might take away your BMW and your hair might turn green and… and… and… Does this sound like the voice inside of your head? Doesn't it wear you out? Doesn't it make you so tired, scared and lonely that there is no energy left to do the things that would move you toward freedom?

See how knowledge, left unfocused, can be downright ridiculous. He runs off in any direction we let him. What is the solution to stop this run away voice in our heads? Focus on who you are, only the facts, and avoid the waffles.

HERE ARE A FEW THINGS I KNOW:

- We're truly afraid of someone taking our things away from us. When you are naked you don't have to hold on to things, you let them go. Everything will come back to you in many ways.

- We're afraid of both success and failure because they both mean something different in our lives. Both mean change and both impact many areas. We fear change because we assume that things are as good as they ever will be. If we get lucky enough to have a great experience, we want to hold on to it forever, in case nothing is ever as good again.

• We're afraid that if we open ourselves up and give of ourselves, we'll run out of things like love, happiness and joy. We're not sure where they come from so we're afraid to share the amount that we have.

You've done work on your naked story. You found out that you actually are at your core a human being (shocking). You do have compassion for fellow human beings (shocking), and sometimes you don't show it at all. When you make cold and harsh decisions that impact others' lives negatively, you delude yourself and think you didn't have a "choice." You might hoard your good feelings for the day and avoid anyone who has a problem for fear that you might "catch" it from them. We're like stingy 3 year olds, clinched up and closed down protecting our favorite "toys," our feel goods. Sometimes you don't want to share because you like having something that someone else doesn't have—it makes you feel special. Tough love here, "you big baby." You don't want to share your toys. You don't want to risk losing your little "love" buzz of feeling good for the day. I've got two words for you when you get to this place and hear these words "Get Naked." You need an AHAA moment. You need to acknowledge it, handle it, apologize and then accept it, and move onward and upward in your relationships. Be still, look inside, ask yourself, "what am I afraid of?" What am I currently attached to (afraid of losing)? What can I open up to? What can I give? Then you need to take the leap and get naked.

Give when you don't want to and see what happens. Acknowledge to the universe "this feels crappy and I have no idea why I have to do this, BUT I trust and I'm going to be present and ignore "know it all" and fall into it anyway and see what happens. You'll be surprised at what can happen at unexpected naked moments. You know you have a choice and wisdom knows why you're in this particular moment, don't listen to knowledge, feel the wisdom flow to you and through you, in the present and now. Let yourself be uncomfortable.

THE ART OF BEING UNCOMFORTABLE

Is getting naked uncomfortable? Uh, yeah, especially at first. I am a student of being uncomfortable. It often reveals a naked opportunity. I haven't always been this way. Remember the beginning of getting naked is recognizing this feeling, the one of anxiety, a squirmy, unnamed discontent. We used to respond with serve and protect, avoid the conflict, conveniently ignore the situation and hope that it would go away. Now I intentionally stay aware of when I'm feeling uncomfortable and try to get more naked. I've found this process to be like wiggling a loose tooth, it's uncomfortable, yet you keep wiggling it because you know it will eventually come out which will ease the pain. Sounds simple, but it's not easy. It does get easier with practice. One way I practice is to talk to strangers, especially when I don't want to. It's really easy to do it when you feel like it. Open up to a stranger. You will probably never see them again, so what do you have to lose? Make them talk to you. Our world is so closed up, cocooned and straight-jacketed. We are numb to each other, start by making eye contact, say an honest hello and make a true statement and see what happens. This is called "conversation" and it builds relationships.

Last winter I was in a very low place. I was in stage 3 melt down and I was no longer able to ignore the frost warnings, the brain freeze or the hypothermia I was in. I was getting on another airplane to go see a client who was not happy. It was the week after Thanksgiving and I was feeling like no one loves me, I have no friends, blah, blah, blah, get the picture? I picked my blonde ponytail head up off the bathroom floor after crying for an hour while laying on the bathroom floor of yet another hotel because the world has not met my expectations on my timeline. I convinced myself that tomorrow would be a better day. I felt good for the two minute walk to the bed where I covered my head and said, as loud as my brain could handle, "this sucks! How did I get here? This is not supposed to be my life! Where's my prince charming? Where's my sash and tiara?" This is not really what I was thinking, but it might as well have been.

There's an ongoing battle between "know it all" and wisdom you know. One of my favorite parables is about the sun and the wind trying to get the man to take his jacket off. The wind blows and blows but to no avail, the man will not remove his jacket. The sun very gently warms him and he easily takes the jacket off. I've always thought myself to be pretty resilient and when the wind blows and blows I just know that sun is going to shine any minute. But at this point in my life, I was pissed at the rain and the sun and I didn't really care a flip about either one of them.

So I met with the client and presented our honest response to their requests and concerns. I absolutely told the truth. I couldn't lose my job at this point, for Pete's sake! If I had lost my job I would have had no reason to get out of bed, except my son, who loved his dad and wants to be with him anyway—I knew that because he told me all the time!

After the meeting the next morning, I dragged myself cheerily to the airplane at 6:30 am to fly back to "nothingness." I got on the plane and thought of my counselor at home who was coaching me to be comfortable being uncomfortable. "Talk to strangers," she said, "you'll never see them again." In order to do this I started playing the airplane game. I cut a deal with God—if he gave me the grace and relief from this pain to make it through yet another day I would intentionally pay attention to the person beside me on the plane. It was a captive audience, short time frame, it couldn't kill me. So this morning I was beside a very large lady, visibly uncomfortable in the small standard seat, and she looked a little bit harsh. Now, not many people look warm and friendly at 7 am and I am ultra sensitive to people who look a little harsh (mean), but I hung in there anyway. I have a problem with mean people, or people who I think are mean, I usually sense their negative energy and really really want to ignore them. At this moment, on this airplane, I think, "really God?" But damn it, I have nowhere to go but up from the bathroom floor I've been wallowing on, so I started talking about the sunrise through the airplane window being the highlight of the trip and she agreed. No conversation yet, just an agreement. I had to work harder to actually converse. I asked her whether she was coming back to Knoxville or going to Knoxville. She said she was visiting her daughter for her granddaughter's birthday party. We had polite small talk about kids and grandkids and she really started to warm up, and then she started to tell me about what a tough time her daughter was having. I was feeling a little challenged, a little anxious, a little insincere, knowing that I was playing a "game" with God by listening to this lady. But, the conversation became very personal very quickly.

I've found that the universe knows so much more than we do. Our vision is so small. This lady's daughter was in a terrible domestic situation. Her husband recently kicked her out of their house and his girlfriend quickly moved in. She had an undergraduate and a Master's degree, but no job experience because of staying home while she was raising their children. The mom talked about how hard it was to be so far away and she basically couldn't do anything but support her daughter in moving forward and beginning to recover from this terrible situation. I genuinely opened up to listen to her with compassion for a parent who has to watch her child in pain. I realized how hard it must have been (and still is) for my mom to watch my addict brother make decisions that would put him in danger and separate him from our family. I realized how painful it would be to see my own son, in a type of pain that a parent cannot alleviate. I knew there was nothing I could do but listen, and this was one of the first times I realized that by listening, you don't catch other people's pain. I saw that by physically speaking her pain, part of it was being released. The daughter was terribly distraught and depressed. Although I have never been officially "depressed," I have had some really bad days. No matter how hard you fight with your mind, you just cannot seem to overcome the pain and despair that has crept deep into your soul. It is the darkest and thickest blanket of fog that descends so quickly you cannot even find your bearings. I recommended a book that I recently read on healing and moving forward and wrote the name down with an ink pen I had picked up free from my counselor's office. As a last thought I gave her the pen and thought her daughter might want to call them. At the last moment, I also decided to give her my first name and phone number in case her daughter wanted someone to talk to, maybe grab a cup of coffee. She thanked me and we got off the plane to go out into our own lives. My immediate thought while I got off the plane was, "oh my God, what have I done?" What if she calls me and wants a place to live, what if she calls me and her husband follows us and my family is in danger and now I'm in the middle of a huge drama? You know who was in full force and my life was of course flashing before my very eyes, "Why did I open my big mouth?" I took a few breaths and thought, "I did the right thing. It will be ok, you have to trust people and your intuition." When my heart says open your mouth, I'm going to trust it's safe to open my mouth. I've found it's when my head says open your mouth that I generally have regrets.

I didn't think about this incident again for weeks. I went back to see my counselor and I arrived a little early, which is very unusual. I went ahead and started writing a check for my visit and the counselor walked out. We greeted each other, I looked down at my hand and remembered the lady on the airplane, "remind me to tell you a story about the pen," I said. "I already know the pen story," she replied, "you have no idea what a difference you made in someone's life that day." I was speechless. "By talking to someone you made the difference between life and death." I was stunned. I was just going to recite a story of talking to a stranger, of being uncomfortable and doing it anyway. I listened to a stranger and gave away a free pen. Yeah me! I followed the instructions and talked to a stranger. I never thought I would actually hear from the family. I reflected on the incident as a part of my personal journey. I actually thought the incident had happened for me, to help me see what can happen when we let ourselves be uncomfortable. I found out it wasn't about me at all.

Because I allowed myself to be uncomfortable, it saved someone's life. I was stunned. I was humbled. I couldn't believe it. I'd love to tell you about what happened to that daughter's life long-term, but I have no idea. Due to patient confidentiality, the only thing that my counselor could say was "You saved someone's life". I hope she got naked. I hope she got the help she needed. I hope that the choice she made to live was the best one she has ever made. I hope someday—she finds out about the pen story and this book. But even if she doesn't, it won't matter. What was supposed to happen did. That day, I made the choice to think of someone else's comfort instead of mine and look what happened.

What an important lesson, a generous invaluable gift of insight and wisdom. We beg the universe to show us why, for explanations, for timelines, and every once in a while, we get to see the miracle of that explanation unfold before our eyes. I learned a lesson about faith that day. Just because we don't see the explanation unfold, doesn't mean that it isn't going to unfold. Life is long and complex. All the dots are there and all we really have to do is listen and show up. Faith is knowing that the dots all connect, even if we don't get to see the final picture. Faith is real and concrete. You just have to open your eyes and look for it. You may never know the difference you make in someone's life at any given moment and I think I am glad about that. If you had that knowledge, just think of the burden that would be to bear. Talk about an appointment that you would worry about missing! You would feel such responsibility and pressure to make sure that you met that obligation. We were not meant to worry about it. We were meant to follow, to have a clear heart and mind and open up to the world, this also means you never know when someone's going to make a difference in yours.

Coincidences, ever had an airplane ride like this? Think about the details, what happened, how did you feel? What were the outcomes of your experience?

Do you actively seek these experiences out? Are you open to them? These are naked adventures; we get to choose to participate. You don't have to plan the adventures, they find you.

NAKED HAS NO EXPECTATIONS

This is a huge one. Some days I really hate this part of naked, it's one of the hardest parts of being in that boat. Expectation has a cousin called patience and they can both be wickedly humbling. I call patience the "P" word because it ends up being the root of the majority of my "wearies." So nakedness reveals that you are indeed human and we struggle with wanting what we want, when we want it. Think about this, we are the inventors of time—we're the only species that has an "official" time. We invented names for the seasons, the months, the clock, and I'm not really sure we have a good reason for it, except so that we could meet other peoples' expectations. The flowers know when to bloom, the birds know when to eat, why did we think we should be able to create our own little "time maps." Ah ha—when we decided we were the "center of the universe" and everything rotated around us. Then we chose to have expectations for others to rotate around us as well and when things didn't come true like we wanted we had the luxury of the self-fulfilling prophecy of failure and we didn't have to deal with that old pesky "purpose for our life" thing. We could then blame other people and anything and everything and whine and cry about what we don't have.

Naked has no timelines, not the same time clocks, not the same pressures from expectations. It waits patiently in the now because wisdom knows that the things that unfold are supposed to be and when we release our expectations and replace them with wonder, we are not disappointed with the outcome or timeline. Naked also can discriminate between the wants and needs and sometimes we need time for us to catch up to that reality.

I struggle with living in a state of expectancy, I know great things are going to happen and I try to have no expectations. I've reconciled the two by realizing that I must not waste time trying to figure out when, where or how things are going to be great. I can't go to the grocery store walking down the aisle thinking Mr. Greatness is going to be around the corner, because when he's not, I'm disappointed. I just go to the grocery store and shop for groceries, with an attitude that great things are in store for me, every day and every where. If I'm only looking for Mr. Greatness, I might miss the buy one get one free special on my favorite cereal and that is a blessing I don't want to miss!

What are your expectations? What's the difference between expectations and dreams? What's the difference between expectations for ourselves and of others? Should you have expectations of others? Do you think you have unconscious expectations of others?

Often our reactions to others reveal our expectations of them. When we get angry because someone doesn't call us, we obviously expected them to call us—why? Because we think they like or love us? So why does that mean they should call? Perhaps it's because that's how we "think" we know they like us? So the only way to know they like you is for them to call? No, I guess I just thought that's what people do when they like you? Think about how much energy and time you have wasted in this time warp vortex in your lifetime. Time spent waiting, hoping and moping. Maybe a residual thought from middle school? So as we look with wonder instead of expectations, see how things change.

Hmm, I wonder why he didn't call. No anger attached, no disappointment, just wonder and then if you want to talk to the person, pick up the phone and call them, this moment, in the present. No strings attached to the past, no emotional reactions. You know you've done the old "Humpf, just thought I'd call to see if you were alive since you didn't take the time to call me" click, hang up. Come on! Be honest, you didn't want to talk at that point, you wanted to inflict pain so they would feel your pain, be dreadfully sorry and of course never, ever do it again. Because they love you, Right? Of course someone who loves you never ever hurts you, right? Uh, wrong! You see "know it all" is very efficient. He stores all kinds of information and categorizes it just in case of an emergency, his recall ability is incredible. But darn that color commentary that he likes to add to everything! He is the perfect boy scout, "always be prepared!"

This is how know it all works. He likes to look for any scenario even remotely close to warn you of potential danger. If you've seen a movie where the guy doesn't call and he's with another girl, of course this fact will be recalled if your boyfriend does not call. So one favor we can do everyone is "don't put them in a movie!" This is funny but really kind of sad and true. I can't imagine the number of arguments and heated discussions the recent movie "The Hangover" spawned. Come on, we laughed whole-heartedly at the movie and inside we thought "he/she" better never do that to me and to make sure, we tested them in some crazy and demented way, which probably did not work out the way you wanted it to. (I believe I threw a water bottle at someone through their car window. Of course this was effective at solidifying their stereotype of the insecure, drama queen women that are everywhere.) We're human, be honest, be naked. Acknowledge that you do this, apologize where you need to and then accept it by being aware and moving beyond it. You will see your relationships improve dramatically. Drama will virtually disappear as it is a reactionary emotional display, you can eliminate it if you want to.

BUILD YOUR NAKED MUSCLES

We talked about baby steps to getting naked. It does become easier and more natural. It follows the natural learning process:

1. Unconscious incompetence: I don't know I'm not naked.

2. Conscious incompetence: Oops, I know I'm not naked, but I don't know how to get naked.

3. Conscious competence: I know I'm not naked, but I'm actively practicing being naked.

4. Unconscious competence: I live a naked life, honest in my thoughts, words and actions.

While you are learning to live in a naked life, be kind and loving to your naked self. Be aware of the things that will happen (re-entry wounds) and choose to stay naked. You might consider the following:

Have a naked night with friends. This is a very light hearted get together, almost like a grown up truth or dare party. You can each write a naked question down, put them in a hat and each draw one out and answer it. You must remember a couple of key naked rules: no gossip, no prodding and no laughing at, only laughing with. This should be safe and fun. It's just a great time to test those magnets and build better connections, slowly. Only invite safe people and this may mean not inviting your mother (or any relatives actually)!

Only buy Christmas gifts for people you want to. Hmm, no more gifts of obligation, last minute gifts from Walgreens or re-gifts from last year. If there is a list of people you just have to buy for that you don't want to, evaluate those relationships and be honest—they are not naked! Either seek to build the relationship or cut bait.

Send a few naked notes per week, to anyone! A naked note is just an honest observation for no reason. It shows someone else you're changing from the inside out. No self-help change of the week, this is the real stuff. It shows you're changing and you should really be proud of that. Remember the rule about not ignoring the nudge to get naked? If someone crosses your mind, stop for a moment and think about it. Maybe they need an apology or a thank you or congratulations. Make room for spontaneous love in your life, that's a naked life.

Don't make commitments you don't intend to keep. Baby showers, graduations, if you aren't going to go, recognize it, be honest and don't commit. You might want to think about why they invited you any way. Don't just assume they want money or a gift. Maybe they respect you, or maybe you're an inspiration to them. Regardless, don't assume, seek to understand why they asked you to go, take a deep breath and follow your heart.

JOIN THE
NAKED MOVEMENT

Now you have a choice: you can join the movement and relish being your naked self, or you can be that person who keeps looking for themselves, out there somewhere. You can keep buying those self-help books, keep joining Weight Watchers, and keep complaining about your spouse, or you can choose a different life.

Look at your bookshelves. What are your books about? What have you been trying to learn, who have you been trying to be? Look at every book and magazine, what sticks and what makes your heart tingle? Where does your naked self want to go and what does that naked adventure look like? If a book doesn't stick to your naked self, move it on its journey. Put in on someone else's path. You are the leaner, meaner, naked you and when you dream about something, you make it come true. Now instead of having shelves of stuff reminding you of what you should do, could be and haven't done, you have tools. You have friends, you have support. Love them, read them, and know them. See what happens when you read these books now. I bet you make things happen—your things, your dreams, no one else's.

I bet your life changes forever.

join the naked movement

www.TheNakedExecutive.com

Everyday

Receive daily insight and inspiration as a fan of The Naked Executive on facebook. Our discussions offer a safe place to tell others how you feel and to see that you are never alone.

Each Month

Become a Naked Movement member at www.thenakedexecutive.com to receive the monthly newsletter filled with motivation and inspiration from other naked members.

Sign Up

Gain access to naked tips and tools at the website as you grow and begin your naked journey.

about the author

Kelly Davies, The Naked Executive, knows how to transform people's lives by applying common coroporate change management strategies learned while gaining her MS in Executive Leadership and Organizational Change from Northern Kentucky University.

She discovered that when we are honest about our fears and feelings, they evaporate- losing their control over us. We are then free to become Naked: honest in our thoughts, actions and words. This freedom allows us to finally build the life of our dreams and accomplish our goals once and for all.

As VP of Operations for CBIZ Medical Management Professionals, she has the opportunity to coach people and practices to success. Serving on the Executive Board for the CBIZ Women's Advantage Program has allowed her to not only provide leadership to other female professionals, but also be mentored and inspired by incredibly talented female leaders within the organization.

When she is not at the ball field with her son, you can find her blogging about life, love and leadership at www.thenakedexecutive.com.

171

BUY A SHARE OF THE FUTURE IN YOUR COMMUNITY

These certificates make great holiday, graduation and birthday gifts that can be personalized with the recipient's name. The cost of one S.H.A.R.E. or one square foot is $54.17. The personalized certificate is suitable for framing and will state the number of shares purchased and the amount of each share, as well as the recipient's name. The home that you participate in "building" will last for many years and will continue to grow in value.

Here is a sample SHARE certificate:

HABITAT FOR HUMANITY

THIS CERTIFIES THAT
YOUR NAME HERE
HAS INVESTED IN A HOME FOR A DESERVING FAMILY

1985-2005

TWENTY YEARS OF BUILDING FUTURES IN OUR
COMMUNITY ONE HOME AT A TIME

1200 SQUARE FOOT HOUSE @ $65,000 = $54.17 PER SQUARE FOOT
This certificate represents a tax deductible donation. It has no cash value.

YES, I WOULD LIKE TO HELP!

I support the work that Habitat for Humanity does and I want to be part of the excitement! As a donor, I will receive periodic updates on your construction activities but, more importantly, I know my gift will help a family in our community realize the dream of homeownership. **I would like to SHARE in your efforts against substandard housing in my community!** *(Please print below)*

PLEASE SEND ME _____ SHARES at $54.17 EACH = $ $_____

In Honor Of: _____

Occasion: (Circle One)   HOLIDAY   BIRTHDAY   ANNIVERSARY

OTHER: _____

Address of Recipient: _____

Gift From: _____ *Donor Address:* _____

Donor Email: _____

I AM ENCLOSING A CHECK FOR $ $_____ PAYABLE TO HABITAT FOR HUMANITY **OR** PLEASE CHARGE MY VISA OR MASTERCARD *(CIRCLE ONE)*

Card Number _____ Expiration Date: _____

Name as it appears on Credit Card _____ Charge Amount $ _____

Signature _____

Billing Address _____

Telephone # Day _____ Eve _____

PLEASE NOTE: Your contribution is tax-deductible to the fullest extent allowed by law.
Habitat for Humanity • P.O. Box 1443 • Newport News, VA 23601 • 757-596-5553
www.HelpHabitatforHumanity.org